Dare to be Authentic
Vol. 5
Let Yourself Prosper

Mari Mitchell with contributing authors

DEDICATION

I dedicate this book to all those who are searching for prosperity. Whether it be in finances, relationships, health, spirituality, or any other area of your life. My desire is that these true and heartfelt stories will encourage and inspire you to take the path you are shown to your prosperity.

Suzanne,

I love that I can share my first publication with you. I pray you will find the writings in this book enlightening.

Dare to be your authentic self and prosper!

Love you,
Jen McDermott

CONTENTS

ACKNOWLEDGMENTS

I thank and acknowledge every author who has written their story for this book of inspiration and encouragement:
Karen Bryce
R. Joan McDermott
Alan Eschenberg
Cheryl Honc
Carmen Ventrucci
Lisa Manzo
Cesar R. Espino
TJ Jordan
Angela Day
Michael Jay Hollander
I applaud your courage in sharing your true and heartfelt story of what obstacles you overcame, in order to proper in your life. May more and more prosperity in all areas of your life, come to you

Karen Bryce

CHAPTER 1
My Unfolding Journey of Authenticity -
Unconditional Self-love and Acceptance

To be nobody-but-yourself - in a world which is doing its best, night and day, making you everybody else—means to fight the hardest battle which any human being can fight; and never stop fighting. - E.E. Cummings

I call myself The *Self Luv Junkie* because I believe wholeheartedly that unconditional self-love, unconditional self-acceptance, and knowing your human worth are the main ingredients for a truly successful and fulfilled life. They are not the only ingredients, but they create a strong foundation, a base where true self-realization and transformation can begin. Why do I believe that statement so strongly? Because of my own past struggles with unconditional self-acceptance, self- love and knowing my worth from the inside out. Unconditional self-acceptance is such an important first step to any change, that it is the essential building block of many recovery programs. Once there is acceptance of reality and themselves in that moment, they can begin to work on changing the things they can change.

No amount of self-improvement can make up for any lack of self-acceptance. - Robert Holden

My emotional struggles stemmed from my childhood experiences of abandonment, having difficulty learning in school, and having to deal with a skin disorder called vitiligo at the age of eleven. What is vitiligo? It's a lack of skin pigment; my immune system is destroying the color of my skin by leaving white patches. It's not a life threating disorder but it can have an emotional, social, and physiological effect on your life. It effects how you see yourself and how you think others see you. It can affect your self-esteem and self-worth. (A famous person who had vitiligo was Michael Jackson and one who has vitiligo is Winne Harlow).

Because of my experiences with these issues, I have learned that if you don't have a strong foundation that you water and nourish every day, life's circumstances can break you down. This can lead you to make unhealthy choices to deal with the mental, emotional, spiritual, and physical pain that these experiences may cause.

Self-acceptance is my refusal to be in an adversarial relationship to myself. - Nathaniel Brander

The combination of these childhood experiences created some very negative beliefs about myself, others, and life. These beliefs left me feeling:

- Empty emotionally
- Not good enough.
- Sometimes depressed, insecure,
- Self-conscious of what people thought of me or how they saw me.

- Always trying to be perfect.
- Comparing myself to others.
- Jealous and creating an internal protective wall by making up stories in my head when it came to my personal and social relationships.
- Afraid to step out of my comfort zone.
- Afraid of speaking my truth
- Like I didn't have a voice.

But on the outside I looked like I had it all together. I kept a smile on my face, saying the right things, not putting myself out there, fearing the truth could be discovered. I made sure to look pretty and perfect. I craved attention and compliments from others so I could feel good about myself. I needed to hear how pretty or beautiful I was. If I went somewhere and didn't get a compliment or attention, I felt that something was wrong. Back then there was no social media to do that for me.

I desperately needed other's people validation so I could feel good about myself, which was short lived once that moment was over. Then I was looking for the next compliment to fill that void.

This is how I lived most of my life - looking outside of myself for everything I needed to feel worthy, comparing myself to others, judging and putting myself and others down in my mind so that I could feel good about myself. I was living in a prison of my own making, participating in life, going through the motions, but so disconnected from my true authentic self. I was trying to live up to an image or standard that I thought would make me happy and cure all of my limiting beliefs about myself.

The thing that is really hard, and really amazing, is giving up on being perfect and beginning the work of becoming yourself." - Anna Quindlen

I was content with playing small and carrying around my baggage, protecting myself, and not letting others pass the wall. But deep down inside I felt empty, I felt that something was missing. I would feel my body's uncomfortable reactions to my negative beliefs, but I would ignore them, put a band aid on them. I was living the Iceberg metaphor. When you look at an iceberg you can only see the top of it floating on the water, but below is a massive portion that is not visible. In my life everyone could see the "perfect" me that I portrayed, but underneath or inside, where no one could see, was the pain, insecurities, negative core beliefs, and the feelings of not being good enough.

Under all of those layers however, there was a strong desire that I was supposed to be doing more with my life than just playing small. That desire was so strong I pushed myself and started chasing the things I thought I was *supposed* to do to bring me that good enough feeling and fulfillment I was craving for.

So, I started jumping from career to career trying to find the right fit. I became a flight attendant, but that was short lived. I then when to school to become massage therapist, but that interest also didn't last very long. I went into skin care and became a makeup consultant. Then I thought I wanted to be in hotel management. I later worked for a weight loss company. Finally, I worked in customer service.

But, still no connection, no fulfillment, no feeling any happier or content like I thought I would. What was I missing? I was so frustrated, I was tired of running and chasing, of feeling stressed out and disappointed when none of my careers worked out. That deepened my not good enough feelings. I felt like I needed to just stop chasing. So, I made a decision that I would leave my very stressful job as a customer service rep and take a less stressful job at a carwash manufacturing plant because I needed something easy with no stress. I wanted to stop this mindless chasing.

Because one believes in oneself, one doesn't try to convince others.
Because one is content with oneself, one doesn't need others' approval.
Because one accepts oneself, the whole world accepts him or her.

- Lao Tzu

Best decision I made, because it seemed like that quiet and peace was what I needed to listen to my heart. It took me a few years sitting there just waiting for something, not sure what I was waiting for, but knowing I had to be still. Then one day I was watching Oprah and she had spiritual teachers, motivational speakers, and life coaches on her show. I was connecting to the messages they were sharing on a deep level. It was like something inside of me already knew this information, like it was a more of remembering what I forgot.

I started listening to motivational speakers, buying self-help books and cd's, taking courses, attending seminars. I became a sponge. I probably could have had a house or nice nest egg in the bank by now with the amount of money I spent looking and searching for the answers, but I was desperate to be free. I did this for years, reading everything that I could get my hands on. I copied hundreds of articles. I was hungry and I couldn't stop. Every time I read or heard something I would feel connected to the information. My soul already knew what I was just waking up to.

Even though I felt a deep connection with what I was reading or hearing, I was not ready to do the work. I got excited about reading a new book, then started it and went through a few chapters, but I didn't finish it. Then I moved on to the next and did the same thing over and over again. I also did the same with the courses and seminars. I felt an almost instant block to going any further because I would have to take responsibility and do the work that was required for me to change.

Deep inside I would feel good about the info, but I would always go back to my old behaviors and patterns, because it was still easier for me to stay in my mess and be a victim. It was easier to let my mind master me, instead of me choosing how I wanted to live and how I wanted to show up in my life. Everything I was reading and listening to was telling me I had to go in and do the work. But hell no, not me, I was going to skip the work and just use this information to create an ideal image of myself, so I could impress others with how much I knew.

You can succeed if nobody else believes it, but you will never succeed if you don't believe in yourself. - William J. H. Becker

With all the "wisdom" I gained I decided that I was ready to become a Life Coach, because I knew everything I needed to know to "fix others" so they could live their best life. I went to school and got my life coaching certification then started my own coaching business. Talk about putting the cart before the horse! I was very proud of myself because I actually finished something I started. Yes! I was ready to help people to change their lives. I was going to tell them what to do, because now I was qualified and I was ready to talk the talk.

As time went on, I realized I was not connecting with my clients. I was repeating information, but something was missing. I felt like it was all on the surface, that I was being fake with myself and with them. I would share information to help them, but there was still pain and disconnection within myself. I felt they were not connecting at a deeper level to themselves. How could they, when they had a coach that was guiding them, but was not connected to her true self. A coach who was living from some ideal image she created and was clueless of the truth.

We can never obtain peace in the outer world until we make peace with ourselves. - Dalai Lama XIV

So of course, what did I do? I kept on searching for more information that would help me connect with my clients. Then one day I came across this statement in an article. "Divine Essence, the truth of who we are is buried deep within our being. We must work our stuff out, if not we spend the rest of our life searching and seeking for things outside of ourselves to fulfill us, that's already within us." - Unknown

That statement was my aha moment. For days I kept looking and repeating that statement. As I did, I felt like that message was starting to break down some walls. I started crying uncontrollably, because I knew that it was about something deeper than what I could see right in front of me. I couldn't put it into words what was happening to me internally, but I knew it was time to do the work, connect with my internal self, and heal.

The privilege of a lifetime is being who you are. - Joseph Campbell

Once I accepted that reality, it came down hard and fast. The flood gates opened up and I started questioning what I thought I knew I had the answers to. How could I have had the answers if:

- I didn't know who I was from the inside out
- I didn't like what I saw in the mirror.
- I had negative beliefs about myself, my body, and my life.
- I was holding on to unforgiveness, anger, pain, resentment, insecurities.
- I was defining myself by vitiligo.
- I was comparing myself to others and not feeling good enough.
- I was accepting less than I deserve.
- I was stuck in my comfort zone.
- I was following a programing of how I was "supposed" to be, act, look, have in order to feel that I have worth.
- I was defining words like happiness, success, inner peace, fulfillment, love, beauty, spirituality,

freedom, prosperity by the standards and programming of others, society, media, family and friends.

- I was disconnected from my divine essence.
- I was disconnected from mind, body, spirit, and from my connection with others, nature, and the universe.

Nothing could have prepared me for the shift that was about to take place in my life by asking myself those powerful questions and letting go of what I thought I knew to be true. Nothing could have prepared me for how this would set me free and set me on a course I never expected. I read this quote, "Once the student is ready the teacher will appear" - Buddha

So true because once I opened myself and let go, the Universe/God/Source/ Infinite Intelligence whatever you call that Power that's greater than us, started sending everything I needed to evolve in all areas of my life. And apparently that growing and evolving never stops because as I write this chapter I am in the process of growth. They said wisdom is when you say, "I don't know." Well, I have been saying that a lot lately. This change didn't happen right away, it has been a journey of constant evolving and being open to life.

I found in my research that the biggest reason people aren't more self-compassionate is that they are afraid they'll become self-indulgent. They believe self-criticism is what keeps them in line. Most people have gotten it wrong because our culture says being hard on yourself is the way to be. - Kristen Neff

I learned that the divine essence never changes, we were born with it and we will die with it. That divine essence honors the depth of who we are, it nourishes our hearts and minds, it empowers us to be our authentic self. That same divine essence created the universe and that force is within us and within everything that has being created.

That divine essence is not stagnant, our authentic self is not stagnant. It grows and evolves and drives our exploration in every area of our lives, in every stage of our lives: work/career, relationships, play, spirituality/faith, friends, fashion, lovers, locations, living arrangements, community, passion/purpose, family. Our authentic self is not one dimensional, there are many parts to us that make up this beautiful whole.

Option A: Spend your life trying to get others to accept you. Option B: Accept yourself and spend your life with others who recognize what a beauty you are. - Scott Stabile

Stepping into our authentic self involves having a strong foundation of complete acceptance of all our parts. We must strive to love those parts, the good and the not so good parts, without qualifications, conditions or exceptions. We must use all parts of us; our shadow side, our thoughts, our feelings, to discover who we truly are from the inside, so that we are not trapped in an existence that's not our own. At the end of the day we can either have regrets or satisfaction based largely on whether we were true to ourselves. The authentic self is the essence of who we truly are underneath all the outward trappings that we believe make us who we are and gives us worth.

You're already stuck with yourself for a lifetime. Why not improve this relationship? - Vironika Tugaleva, "The Art of Talking to Yourself"

Having that strong foundation is NOT about being self-centered, arrogant, comparing self to others, egotistic, rude, selfish, judgmental, always winning, looking down on others, perfect, or looking after number one. It's about allowing for the fullest potential of who you are to come alive and for that divine essence that's within you to shine that light and energy through you, so your light can benefit the world. That light has an extremely important impact and purpose in the lives of others and on this planet.

Our authentic self is that light. That light is already perfect in its imperfections and any reason that holds us back from that type of love is completely false. We were programed to believe that if we have enough, do enough, get enough, be enough, it defines who we are. We were told that all this would fulfill us and make us happy, but we are waking up to fact that it's not enough.

Who are we without the accolades, the degrees, the achievements, society's images of success, money, cars, houses, clothes, kids, spouse, outer beauty, etc. If we were stripped of everything that we think makes us who we are, who would we be? Don't get me wrong, there is nothing wrong with stuff and the outside trappings, this life is meant to be enjoyed and lived to the fullest. The problem is when it defines who we are, when we look down on others, when we judge others, compare, when we become greedy, jealous, when we destroy others, when we are obsessed with perfection, when it disconnects us from source and our true self.

Just look around at what's happening in the world, we have loss our connection to something greater than ourselves, we have lost connection to who we truly are, we have loss connection to each other, we have lost our connection to this magnificent planet. Because we have forgotten our true purpose for being here as a collective, we have become disconnected, divided by race, religion, money, greed, status, boarders, politics, looks, etc.

In order for any changes to take place in the world it has to start with each of us first. We have to look into the mirror and be honest about the things within us that we need to change. And really it not about fixing ourselves, it is about remembering that we have always been whole, perfect, and complete. We just forgot that truth about ourselves.

Reconnecting with our true divine essence, our magnificence, is that strong foundation that will set us free from the stories that we keep replaying that dictates our beliefs, thoughts, feelings, choices, and what we attract in our lives. In order for this change to take place and to continue to take place we must go from non-acceptance to acceptance, to unconditional self-love, to understanding our human worth.

For me, this shift didn't happen right away. It has taken me a long time to finally grasp my worth, because the negative beliefs and programming were so engraved in me. I had to look at what was not working more than what I needed to change. I also realized that the path to growth will not always be walking through a garden of flowers and butterflies, growth doesn't occur when we are comfortable.

In order for me to prosper spiritually, mentally, and emotionally it was necessary for me to allow myself to be in that uncomfortable space, until I began stepping into my authentic self.

We don't have to wait until we are on our deathbed to realize what a waste of our precious lives it is to carry the belief that something is wrong with us. - Tara Brach, *Radical Acceptance*

Karen Bryce is Creator/Facilitator of A Journey To Your Authentic Self Program and creator of various transformational groups for women: Sister Circle, Women Inspiring Women To Greatness and Soulful Self Luv Coaching. She's also co-creator of A Woman's Journey. Karen's passion is supporting women on their journey of connecting to their true dive essence, understanding the mind body soul connection, shifting consciousness and the effects that their own internal healing can have on others and the planet. Karen's services are available world-wide via phone, video conference, or in person.
Phone: 954-305-9933 email: secoachkaren@gamil.com
Facebook: Soulful-Selflove Coaching IG: soulful_selfluv

R. Joan McDermott

CHAPTER 2
Life's Journey Through Authenticity

The title of this book is daunting and challenging. Daring to be my authentic self in public? I felt it triggering such resistance in me. As I sat with this in quiet reflection I struggled with the discomfort of exposure of my soul's intimacy with my Creator. This is such a curious phenomenon. After all, my seven year old heart's desire was to turn people on to the great love of this awesome God. I remember dancing in the sunshine one day and looking up at the sky saying, "Oh God, if people only knew how wonderful you are, their lives would be so much better."

By the time I reached my junior year in high school I had two dreams rattling around in my heart. One was to become a nun so I could tell the whole world my discovery of a loving God. The other was my dream of being a singer in a band. It was shortly after my Junior Prom, Ma saw me writing my repertoire on the back of my brother's shirt cardboard. Curiosity got the best of her and she asked "What are you doing Joanie?" I proudly declared that the band leader at my Junior Prom liked my singing. (I had actually asked him if I could sing a song with them.) I explained that when I finished he gave me his card and wanted me to come for an audition and bring my repertoire. Well, Ma had a declaration of her own. "No daughter of mine is getting into that business, so just rip it up."

I was shocked and hurt. I tried to tell her how good I was and how much he liked me. My mother explained what a rough way of life that would be. Her declaration was final. I was devastated and angry, but when all was said and done, I had to admit I had become kind of scared about the kind of life I might get caught up in.

Soon my original dream to become a nun emerged. I figured that it would be the best vehicle to tell the world about this loving God of mine. The thought of it became stronger as each day passed. One day while at my friend's house, I decided to talk with my ninth-grade teacher. I picked up the phone and called up the convent. I got right down to business and asked her how a person became a nun. She told me all the details of entry into the convent, and was surprised to hear that I was the person who wanted to become a nun. I couldn't wait to get home and tell my mother. I smiled when she said, "Well, let's see what your father has to say about that."

Pa acted surprised at my news. He asked if I knew it was a hard life and questioned me about whether this was something I really wanted to do. I was very convinced about everything and he could see and hear my joy and determination. So he hugged me and looked me straight in the eye saying, "Well, Joanie, if you become a nun, be a good one," and he hugged me.

Ma and I got busy with buying the list for my dowry. There were two things on the list we bought that made me laugh; a corset and a pair of "old lady" shoes. I was thin and didn't need a corset, and why on earth did I need to wear shoes like my mother wore. It was fun shopping with my mother. Actually that was only true for me. Ma's anxiety around money revealed itself with her admonition that she didn't want to be spending all this money on me just to have me enter the convent and then leave. I have ten brothers and three sisters. Having a family of fourteen children must have sent a ripple down my mom's spine as she spent so much money on her thirteenth child. I understand that now, but all I heard back then was her annoyance. In typical teenage fashion I shot back at her how I had been working since I was fifteen and handed her my signed paycheck and only got two dollars back to use for spending money. Then I finished my angry tirade by telling her what she could do with her money. I expected to get a slap and was surprised to hear her simply state, "Listen to the mouth on you, and you want to be a nun."

The day arrived. I smoked my last cigarette on the way up the curvy mountainous road that led to the novitiate. The street that led to the front door was lined with trees and was beautiful and welcoming. As we climbed the stairs to the dormitory after our last visit with our families, I heard the weeping of the other postulants and was puzzled by it. My heart was exploding with my love for God and knew I was really home! Nothing but joy filled my heart.

I will not say that the next eighteen years were filled with the same kind of exultant love and joy. There was so much to do, learn, and adjust to. I will say that I always carried in my innermost self a deep knowing I was where I truly longed to be. Living in community was not always easy. There were so many different personalities, and we all had the same painful experiences of the rub of our defective histories. It was hard for me to discover that we did not always act kindly to each other. I also remember hitting a spot of darkness. I didn't understand that in such a major transition there is a place of depression. It frightened me and I didn't know how to talk about it. I had always found my way through confusion. My most effective tool was denial. Somehow that wasn't quite as effective anymore.

The darkness in my heart passed but I was still left with the inability to understand. Sometimes it takes years to put the pieces together. I have to confess that I appreciate that gift of not knowing everything all at once. The gradual education and revelation keeps the stream of life flowing a little more smoothly. There was so much more that was being woven together in those eighteen years of spiritual bliss. I was growing more in love with God. I love the safety and simplicity of a life of good orderly direction. The education I was receiving filled me with fullness and joy. The externals were not always comfortable, but doable and many times sheer delight.

As the days, weeks, months, and years flew by, my spiritual life deepened. The ability to move with grace through some very difficult circumstances was a work in progress. By the time I was finally professed, I was a new teacher and was looking forward to my first "mission". It turned out to be a school in North Providence, Rhode Island. One of the sisters I lived with there used to be my fourth-grade teacher. We were a handful in those days and I felt awful about the way we fourth graders used to treat her. She was very kind and affectionate toward me. It was a nice surprise, because I thought she was a crazy old nun when she was my teacher. I found out that she suffered from depression.

The cook in that convent was a lover of animals, not people. I discovered that she was an active alcoholic. Underneath her grumpy ways she was sweet and kind. This ability to see the goodness in others turned out to be one of my best gifts. When I think about it, that insight carried me through many difficult experiences. My contrasting side was getting by the criticism of others. It was painful and I kept it all to myself. Growing into authenticity is a day at a time life-long awakening. Writing this chapter is a wonderful way of opening my inner box of hidden wounds.

The "Nunnery" powers that be, seemed to discover that I was quite adaptable and so I was moved to a different place every couple of years. When I was moved to the little town of East Greenwich I was charmed by the beauty of the place. There was a very long lovely street called Love Lane. I really loved to walk along that street that so deserved its name. The homes looked like mansions and they were enclosed behind low rock walls. It was like being in heaven. The flowers, trees, and decorated lawns were breathtaking and I felt such serenity and peace as I strolled along, just soaking in what I had never seen or felt in the city.

I met a beautiful woman on those walks. She had been sick (cancer I think) and was out looking at her gardens. We started a conversation and I discovered her love for God and her deep faith. One day when I came home from one of these walks, I was questioned by my superior about whether I had finished all my chores. I replied with full innocence to all of her questions. I remember knowing inside that she was stressed and overwhelmed and I was trying to make her feel better by telling her my story of the wonderful walk I had just experienced. She let me know it was not something I should be doing. In those days we always traveled by twos. I thanked her even though I was annoyed at her raining on my parade.

When I was changed from East Greenwich to another mission, Sister wrote me a very loving note thanking me for my kindness to her while I was living there. It touched my heart that she recognized that part of me that simply loved those in need and I know she needed a little extra kindness. Not many of the sisters living there liked her, if any. Of course, this was also revealing the codependency that would plague me.

Next, I was sent to a very large combination of convent and school. It was a boarding school and very official looking. This was very different from anywhere I had lived. There was a bridge from the school to the convent. We lived on the side with the girls that were boarding there. Now that was a challenge. I remember the day we had some drunken sailors roaming the halls. The girls were scared and didn't know how to get them to leave. I happened to be in that area and saw the situation. It seemed so natural for me to speak to the sailors in a friendly way and have a sense of humor about them being lost in a girls' boarding school. It didn't take long for me to show them the door and send them on their way. I think my easy way with them came from the fact that I had ten brothers and therefore no fear of men who had a few too many.

By the end of my time at Bayview, our Sisters of Mercy were having many meetings about how to serve people better. We were given permission to choose how we wanted to serve God in this world. If we had special gifts and could find a place to use those gifts, we could ask permission to change our place of living. I toyed with the idea of going to the Child Care Home in Greenville, Rhode Island. When St. Aloysius Home first came into being, it was an actual orphanage. When I received permission to join the ranks there as a Child Care Worker it housed children from broken homes or those needing temporary housing. I was assigned to and became an integral part of the lives of twelve girls ranging in age from six to thirteen. I slept in a room next to their dormitory that had a window between us. This gave me the opportunity to keep a good eye on them. I was in charge of their rising, getting to meals, getting to school, doing chores, playing and getting to bed. It was exhausting. I found ways to get them organized. I let them make the rules themselves. We had meetings and discussions and decisions about what to do if the rules were broken. It was a whole new way for them to live. I decided to learn how to drive so I could take them on shopping excursions on my day off. There was a budget and they knew what they could buy and had to keep within the allotted budget. Meanwhile, we could talk in the car and get to know each other. All of it worked. They went from calling me *a fucking asshole who didn't even look like a nun and they were going to rip my fucking eyes out of my head*, to becoming a group of girls who were able to help each other and have a somewhat peaceful life.

We caregivers at the Home were given excellent mental health training and supervision as to how to work with the children. This wonderful Clinical Psychologist taught us what to do when the kids got out of control. I believe that the most important lesson I learned from him was that if we truly loved the girls we could not make a mistake. Oh the eternal power of love that always serves us so well.

While loving my work with the girls I was gaining insight into gifts I never knew I had. At the same time I was also coming into greater awareness of the emptiness I had been experiencing. I was missing the presence of my best friend (the previous administrator) and it was eating away my insides. I needed to be able to talk with her. You see, my driving instructor had raped me. After my last driving test preparation, he had suggested we celebrate how well I drove that day. We stopped at a restaurant and he bought me a glass of wine. When I stepped into the rest-room he bought me a second glass. I didn't finish it because it made me feel woozy. I asked him to take me back to my friend's house. When I got to the car, I climbed into the back seat to take a nap. When the car stopped and I awoke, I discovered I wasn't at Joanne's house but in the woods. He climbed into the back seat and was forcing himself on me. I screamed and he stopped. I was shaken and so ashamed. All I could say when Joanne opened the door was that I needed to go to bed. I'm sure I smelled of wine and looked disheveled and shaken. I just wanted to crawl under the covers and I don't remember talking to her about it the next day. I do know that it's true that we are as sick as our secrets.

It was during those two years as a Child Care Worker that I was discovering what the process of grieving was all about. I suffered from feeling abandoned by my friends. What made it worse is the new Administrator didn't seem to like me. I did the best I could to adjust to this, but I began developing resentments, especially when I was denied a ski trip with the other Sisters. They were all excited about it. The reason given why I couldn't go was that I had to stay at the Home and take care of the girls. It felt very personal. My heart was becoming very heavy and my girls were noticing the change in me. They needed me to love and comfort them and my falling into a depressed, distracted state of mind was not at all helpful to them. At that point I asked to be released from my three-year contract. I told the new Administrator that I had to leave. I was so exhausted and needed to figure out what was going on with me. I had never felt this way before. I asked and was given permission to live in our House of Prayer in Cumberland, Rhode Island. The Administrator of the Home gave me some great words of wisdom before leaving. She told me that once I left it was important not to question myself but to keep moving forward. Little did I know those very words would prove to be prophetic.

I found the House of prayer to be just what I needed. I went back to teaching. I loved having eleven girls and eleven boys in a Country Day school. This time I was teaching fifth graders. We did many fun things together. Once we walked up the hill to where I lived. They loved the beauty of the place and we stopped to say a prayer as we made a quiet visit to our little chapel. I had other duties such as getting our retreatants rooms ready, making and serving their meals, and if requested, became their spiritual directors or simply honored their desire to be quiet. It was the place of my dreams. Being run by donation basis only and open to all, the flow of love there was healing in itself.

There were two most significant happenstances during that last year of my life as a sister in our House of Prayer.

One was my discovery of the benefits of a nip and a nap, and the other was the introduction of a holy monk who became our spiritual director. During that time the Charismatic Renewal in the Church was becoming well known. We were letting our non-Catholic brothers and sisters share their way of expressing the movement of the Spirit through their sharing of Scripture and emotionally expressed this stirring in song and raising of hands. It shook us loose and widened our hearts. This singing and moving and shouting out our love was all kinds of joy for me.

The holy monk had been given permission to come out of his cloistered life to check it out. He had come to our House of Prayer as his home base. I found him the perfect person to meet with and try to figure out why I was feeling so differently. I had always loved serving people and helping them through hard times. Each week I would let him know that my feelings were changing dramatically. I didn't want to do it anymore, which was very disturbing to me. I just had to get my act together and figured he could help me.

Meanwhile, I realized that when I came home from school I was very tired. I discovered that if I took a nip of wine and a quick nap, I would be ready to serve our retreatants. I would tell everyone how magical it was. Then I discovered that if I bought a half gallon of wine, it would be more economical. Another great realization that was becoming an occasional treat, was when a priest friend of ours would take Sister Angela and me out to lunch. I noticed they ordered a drink called a Manhattan. The waitress asked if they wanted it with ice or straight up, they chose straight up. All that with a cherry on the top sounded great, so I would order the same. Wow, after drinking a straight-up Manhattan I enjoyed the bonus of a warm fuzzy feeling that made me feel relaxed and wonderful. Each time from then on I would order this mood enhancing drink. Only years later did I realize there was a connection between the progression of warm and fuzzy and wanting more, and being restless, irritable, and discontent.

As the year went on, my beautiful monk, who had become my spiritual director, mentioned that I had been repeating the same trouble with not wanting to serve the people the way I used to and I would have to move on to serve in other places that needed my gifts. I feared that I would not serve well out in an unpredictable world. He made a stunning statement that day that truly rocked my world. He said that he didn't believe God would want me in a form of life that was harmful to me. I thought he was crazy. I never even considered leaving the convent. I thought maybe I had misunderstood until he said, "Now I'm not telling you to leave and I am not telling you to stay. What I suggest you do is sit quietly with your bible in your lap. Then open up all the doors of your mind and heart to the Holy Spirit and don't be afraid of what the Spirit may blow in."

I felt relieved. I was still very prayerful and more than willing to take his suggestion. So obediently I took time to sit quietly in my room with my bible on my lap and a glass of wine in my hand. I closed my eyes, relaxed and opened my mind and heart to whatever God was going to tell me. As I rocked back and forth in my comfortable rocking chair, drinking my wine, I noticed the Spirit was not blowing anything into my mind, so said to God, "You're not telling me anything so this is what I am going to do. I'm going to leave because nobody seems to know what is wrong with me, and you are going to take care of me. Right God?" I then flipped my bible open and it was Zephaniah talking to God's people who had gotten lost along the way. I took the message as though it had been spoken to me. There were three things that would happen if I would just turn back: God would remove my shame, renew me in His love and set me as a light for others. I took this message personally, looked at God in awe and said, "Good deal, God, thank you"!

The next day I began the process of becoming released from my vows. I began searching for a teaching job and place to live. I also began telling the elderly Sisters that I often would visit, of my decision and plans. They were shocked, sad, and concerned for me. They were also comforting in their promises of remembering me and wishing me all the best.

My entry into the world as a secular brought me to the stark realization that I was no longer a nun. I had to find a job and a more practical place to live. There I was with $100 in my pocket, a guitar, and a suitcase with my clothes. I looked like Maria from The Sound of Music. I ended up at Bridgeport University where I became the woman co-chaplain on campus with Father Devore. Next to the Newman Center was the office of the Director of Plant Engineering where a job had opened up that day. It became mine. The Newman Center students told us of a For Rent sign in a window up the street. When we came back, Father announced that I now had two jobs and a home.

How did I land in Bridgeport, Connecticut when I had lived all thirty-six years of my life in Rhode Island? Coming from a large family, everyone had an idea of what I could do with my life. None of their suggestions seemed helpful. I barely understood who I was at that point. My friend Mike from New Haven was there to help me. We had met in St. Bonaventure University when I was getting my Master's in Theology. He was fun to be with and one summer Father Gabe and I were invited to his family's home for a little vacation. Mike was part of our campus ministry students that Father Gabe and I had formed during the summers we were there. The friendships we formed were a big part of our socializing on campus. Thus, the friendship with Mike lasted even after graduation. I was Sister Mary ThereseAnn until the last summer when I actually graduated as Joan McDermott.

A very important element to mention regarding this phase of my life was the continuation of my drinking. I started a group activity with the Newman kids called Wine and Words. They would choose a reading they had found helpful or entertaining, and we would discuss it. During this activity I tried my best not to go to the bar where the wine was too often. I noticed how difficult this had become. The year went on with lots of visits from Mike and lots more drinking in bars after his basketball games. Once he dropped me on my head trying to get me to my apartment. The streets were icy and I was drunk. I blamed him not just for dropping me, but for his taking me to the bars. Why he asked me to marry him was beyond me. He told me he had fallen in love with me when I was still a nun. I never knew that. The day I said yes was after I had been raped by a man on campus who had taken me out to dinner. Mike was caring and attentive to me. The drinking just seemed normal. We did get married after many discussions and some counseling by Father Gabe. I don't know when friendship blossomed into a marrying kind of love, but there I was, married to a third generation undertaker.

We bought a house in North Haven Connecticut. I worked hard on making it beautiful inside and out. During the first five years of our marriage we suffered from six miscarriages. We never were able to have a child. Both of us were progressing into our alcoholism and life was not always pleasant. Ten years into our marriage I decided to get help, so I went to a Recovery program. I knew nothing about alcoholism or that there was a recovery program for people who could not stop after the first drink. I liked the people but thought they were all nuts to even think of stopping completely. I kept going to the meetings, too afraid to drink. I began to identify with their stories. Recovery really began the day I said I was an alcoholic. It was my first awakening to the given reality that offered me a hope.

So much has happened during the past thirty-six years of sobriety. My heart was called back to my love for helping people and I went to school to get my license in Counseling. I started my practice under the title of Counseling, Recovery and Healing. I added Psychotherapy, Master Addictions Counseling and Spiritual Director to my personal development. All was well with me. I was happy. Mike, on the other hand, did not stop in the progression of his disease. He lost himself and everything in his life, including our marriage and his business. We divorced in 2006 and he died suddenly of a pulmonary embolism in 2007. I always loved the goodness of this beautiful man. We helped each other walk through the divorce. It brought back the true love we had for each other. He had divorced me to remove me from legal involvement in the fallout of his alcoholic behaviors. That was a great act of love that I still cherish. Love never fails.

I moved to California in 2008 and have since become a Transitional Life Coach. There is so much more to be revealed. Daring to be my authentic self in this writing has brought me to see both the liar in me and the truth seeker. Our lives are a journey into our own authenticity. Each circumstance, every loss that moves us into change, serves as an opportunity for acceptance. In this acceptance lies the resolution of our grief which reveals the power we gain in our surrender to a given reality. Authenticity is the truth that sets us free.

R. Joan McDermott, TLC, is a Certified Law of Attraction Life Coach, Professional Counselor, Certified Psychotherapist, Master Addiction Counselor, and Spiritual Director. Joan's present title of Transitional Life Coach has developed over the years of major transitions and transformations. From early beginnings the call on her heart has been to bring love and healing to those who struggle through the significant changes in their lives whether brought about by choice or unforeseen circumstances. Today Joan brings the richness of her history into the compassionate love and deep belief in her client's gradual revelation of their emerging dreams.
Email: rjmcdermott54@gmail.com

Alan Eschenburg

CHAPTER 3
LIGHTS, CAMERA, TRANFORMATION

I can't do this anymore…the more I try the worse it gets. I was holding wet blond hair up, blinded by the spotlights from the distance, TV cameras zooming in on my demonstration of the latest hair cut for thousands of hairstylists who had come to my stage show class for one of the top hair brand manufacturers of the world. Blood began oozing onto that beautiful blonde hair, not from a cut from the scissors, but from my hands that were in the final stages of raw skin, eroded away by the chemicals in these so-called natural products. My dream career, one reserved for the finest in the industry and one where I was the youngest ever to do such a prestigious job, now demanded I make a decision about my future. It had to come to an end. My health was more important than the applause, accolades, and money. I wasn't even thirty years old yet and my dream of being a performer all my life had not only come to fruition, but had now died, right in front of my audience.

Growing up in a small town in Texas wasn't easy for

a small, sensitive boy. It was obvious by 1st grade that I was "vertically challenged" and it was looking pretty certain that I did NOT resemble the muscular, dominate male role models on either side of my family. I decided at six years old that being a rancher or oil field worker was never going to happen for me. Doctor? I couldn't stand the sight of blood, so forget about that.

In our family which was riddled with incessant gossip, complaints and bullying, I was continuously reminded that I was a short, little sissy who couldn't do sports and to top it off, came from a divorced family.

Clinging to my granny's side every morning because she was my babysitter who protected me from my uncles, grandfather, and neighborhood kids, I knew that by 3 pm she would have to go to work at the hospital as a nurse. That meant I'd have to endure two hours of terror each of those days under my uncle's or grandfather's ruling. Before that though, I would help her get ready for work. Polish her white shoes, help her iron her uniform, and even style her hair. It was then that I realized for myself that I'd never be a doctor, and maybe my job would be to make nurses look their best so they could do what they do better; helping patients get well.

For the next eleven years, I went to public school. I always got good grades. A few awards here and there, but not until I was eleven years old, did I start my musical training. I loved it. From there, it was pretty clear to me and everyone that musical performance would be my career. Breaking records, I landed a chair in a National Honor Band, thanks to my director whom I believe falsified my age by a year to get me an audition. True or not, I was not just the smallest kid in the orchestra, I was the youngest. I remember the conductor acknowledging us and little did I know that my life would turn from what he said.

"I'm honored to work with such fine musicians, the best of the best. Unfortunately, only one-tenth of one percent of you will make it as well-paid career musicians. So, let's give them a concert they'll never forget." That meant that maybe ONE of all of us was going to make it, and I remember that day deciding I was not going to invest my whole life into being that only one. I had already experienced living hand-to-mouth after my parents' divorce and taking a chance of making it big with those statistics was not for me. I wanted more. I remember saying to myself, "I've got to get a backup plan." It wasn't until my senior year in high school, while braiding a classmate's hair with a line of girls waiting for me to braid theirs, that I realized this might be the money maker I could do while I paid my way through college as a musician.

The day after high school graduation, I drove off from my home to beauty school feeling excited yet at the same time so lonely. It had been very clear that my parents could not afford the college expenses and none of the awarded scholarships were enough to get me through to a degree, so I knew that it was going to be up to me.

I loved beauty school. I got there early, stayed late and even befriended the owner of the school who did hair in the back for her clientele. I was a "human-hair-clip" for her. I swept hair from around her chair and cleaned her area. Before I knew it, I was being hated by the instructors and seniors, because I became Mrs. Conlee's apprentice. I now had the owner of the top private schools in Texas at that time, as my private instructor. She only knew and talked about two things - cooking and hair. I kept the conversation on hair and I did whatever I could to be at her side as much as possible. She and her husband, award winning colorists and stylists, opened their school as a result of great success and wanted to pass their expertise to the industry. I made myself their number one fan, student, and apprentice.

About two months in, Mrs. Conlee told me about a hair show in San Antonio in which platform artists from

London, Milan, Germany, and other countries were going to be teaching. She suggested I go. I had no idea what she was talking about, so I just did what she said. Scrimping every dollar I could, skipping meals, and doing without for a few weeks, I saved enough money to get a ticket to the show. Mrs. Conlee said, "Take a lunch with you, because you will not want to miss a moment." She was right.

My mind was blown as I walked into a huge convention center with tens of thousands of stylists crowding around runway stages, music booming, lights, cameras, and projection theatre screens. The crowd cheered over some of the craziest looking hair on models never before seen at that time. This was being done LIVE by some of the wildest looking characters I had ever seen. It was that very moment I said to myself, "I'm going to be a platform artist!"

I had no idea what it required, what education was needed, who I had to meet, or anything. I had that same feeling in my chest that I'd get as a musician before, during, and after a performance. It was mine. I knew it and I never once tried to figure out how to get there. I knew only one thing for sure. I had to move to a city that had a hub airport, because the platform artists were flown every weekend to another city doing these shows. I had to be airport-ready. That's all I knew for sure and shortly thereafter I moved to Houston, not knowing a single person.

At that time, I had discovered something about life and about myself, which is the way I always gauge how to go about things when I am "manifesting" my life and projects. This "mode" I go into is the same mode that is talked about in so many different ways and the trick to making it work is to not think, *I already heard this before*. In traditional schooling "they" tell you the path to success. In self-help, "they" tell you to make a visual collage, or vision board. In religion, "they" tell you to pray to this or that. What I did looks similar, yet it's distinctly refined. It's what

I've used since then to bring forth every great thing in my life and conversely when I didn't do it, I'd get to a certain point to find that project, idea, or notion fall apart at the seams.

What was so unique about the day I watched those platform artists in the convention center was that I didn't want to be one of them one day. I didn't say, let me go ask my instructor how to become one of them. I didn't run up to one of them onstage or sneak backstage to ask them how to be one of them. I simply said to myself, "I'm a Platform Artist. I am one of THEM." From that moment forward I WAS a Platform Artist.

I went back to beauty school that week and everything I did, I did as if I was a famous platform artist. I acted as if I had brought home Bruce from Manhattan, Heidi from Germany, Xenon of London, and all the performer stylists I watched for two full days at that trade show and they had each given me private lessons. I walked, talked, and even stood and carried on as if I were them. In so doing, I felt more like myself than I had ever felt in my life. Even though I was basically pretending to be THEM, all rolled into one and ultimately into myself.

In retrospect, I for the next few years completely forgot the "voices" of my bullies, mean teachers, uncles, and naysayers. I no longer was trying to escape my past, my insecurities, my fears, my competitors. I ate, drank, and slept hair. I studied, practiced, experimented. I went to every show within driving distance, learning more and more. Having already been the youngest musician, I soon found out that I had quickly become the youngest stylist to climb the ladder of success and performance. It was less than two years from that first show I saw, when I appeared on my own stage. I remember overhearing someone refer to me as "that little boy Platform Artist." I had no idea that you weren't supposed to be on stage until you had twenty to thirty years of salon experience from behind the chair. Good thing.

I ended up working for one of the top companies, flying thirty-six weekends a year to teach seasoned stylists new approaches to haircutting, haircoloring, and styling. I was now in charge of my own productions. I had my shows choreographed, themed, and branded to catapult me within a decade to superstar stylist. I was a sort of *Dougie Howser of Hair.* (Dougie was a teenaged medical doctor on a TV show in the 80's).

Then, one morning as I took my place on stage with my newly blonded model sitting center stage, as I would at any show, I had no idea that this would be the last show for me as a Platform Artist. For a few years I had what was called contact dermatitis. It was a blanket term for itchy skin that was a result of contact from an allergen of some sort. Until that morning though, I had been able to manage it with my doctors by using cortisone creams, gloves, heavy medical moisturizers, occasional injections into each finger, and even sleeping in medications with my hands wrapped in cellophane. I knew that each weekend it would get worse, as I slathered products onto the hair without gloves on my hands. After my two days on stage, I'd use the next five days to medicate and alleviate the itching, swelling and dryness.

That morning, I slathered styling liquid into my model's hair and sectioned off a panel of hair, accepting the usual stinging sensation on my knuckles and between my fingers. I lifted that section of hair above her head to prepare it for creating my cutting "guide line," (This is a measuring "line" in a haircut and becomes the guide of the length of each hair as we do a haircut.) so that my audience could see my work clearly. It was now time to make sure that the TV cameras were able to zoom in on my initial cut. Looking past my fingers to spot the camera, lights blinding my sight, yet shading the glare with my fingers and hair, I know it's aligned. To double check, I turned right to my TV monitor, to make sure I've given my cameraman a perfect shot. As I looked at that perfectly held section of hair ready to be cut, I saw blood trickling down my finger onto that hair. Very distinctly red blood on very blond hair. It was clear to me and to everyone watching that is was NOT from having cut myself with my shears, since I had not cut a single hair yet. In that very moment my career as a Platform Artist was over.

I don't really remember more about that day. I reached over for a towel and my support staff wrapped my finger in Band-Aids. I continued to work till the end of my contracts with the company I worked for, but that was it. They realized it didn't look good to have their demonstrator bleeding in front of their audiences, from using their products. I was devastated to say the least. A performance career of a lifetime, ended by the erosion of my skin from the very products I was showing from the stage.

For the next decade I scoured shows for products that were natural, products that did not sting my hands, as well as products that would alleviate the pain and the scarring that had already become part of my accepted plight. I kept the faith that someone would come along, invent a product that would be safe for me and when that happened, I'd be once again a Platform Artist.

As that decade slammed shut, my sister and I were having an overeating frenzy in the kitchen one evening after "one of those days" in the salon. After a few years of college studying computer programming while working in a pharmacy as a compounding tech to put herself through college, my sister had become a colorist and stylist. It was supposed to be for just the summer that she'd work at our family salon, but it was obvious that the beauty bug had bitten her too. Well, as we were winding down over a cheesecake, we started talking hair of course and came up with an idea. "What if we could feed the hair the way we feed our pie holes?"

With that, we laughed then got down to business. We wrote down food ingredients known for hair use and were adamant that the products had to be silicone-free as well as toxic and chemical free. We figured with my background in the industry and her expertise in pharmaceuticals, we could trace back any chemical to its safe origin and then refine that for use in the hair. It was here again that I forgot my past. I was riveted to my future, a future of healthy hair for everyone using safe food grade perfection without the use of questionable chemicals.

With nothing more than that, we got busy. We experimented, researched, and travelled to find ingredients and with no real or formal guidance. We just kept acting like we were world famous stylists who had invented a new era in the beauty category. "They" laughed at us, told us we were stupid, that we'd never get it done and even if we did, no one would want it. Like my Platform Artistry "ladder of success" was not there, the ladder of success for hair care manufacturing was not there, either.

As if I had just graduated from high school, without letting the past dictating my future, I just kept doing what I knew in my heart was the best and next right thing. We offered to the world our hair products that are silicone-free as well as toxic and chemical free. It's no accident that our company has risen above and beyond in spite of the competition, sabotage, and undermining. Our achievements went from sitting next to our chief formulator on a plane one day, (who ended up refining our formulas beyond world class brands) to a celebrity stylist who found out about our products from a client who demanded our main conditioner, that she brought from home, be used on her, to making our way to the red carpet ourselves with Hollywood's prestigious Makeup Artists and Hairstylist Awards in 2014.

To this day, we not only serve the finest clients in the world, who demand our products for their superior standards; we giggle as we now consider watching TV shows, movies, and entertainment programs part of our job. We have to check the show to make sure our celebrity clients look their best. Not only that, our products are even loved by the set designers and they give us "product placement" in shows. It's unreal to us and yet completely normal at the same time.

After several decades of experience, I now know one thing for sure. When I just allow myself to get caught up in the excitement of something that is truly authentic for me, something takes over. Each of my phases of life, being a musician, a Platform Artist, a hair care manufacturer, seem to be almost unrelated. Yet each has had me in the spotlight somehow. Today, with the challenges that come with manufacturing and creating careers and prosperity for everyone involved, I sometimes wonder if I'm supposed to get ready to retire. So many of my friends are taking their early retirement packages, yet I just don't see it for me. In fact, I'm just getting started because I now have a theory to prove a few more times and for many reasons.

I believe that life is a function of the beliefs that I have collected, sorted, and kept. I also believe I must be informed by the past, yet not limited by it or allow it to be the deciding factor. For example; if I tasted brussels sprouts once and I didn't like them, I could decide I will never try them again. But I wouldn't be taking into consideration that maybe it was a bad recipe that day, maybe I was not hungry, or maybe it was at a restaurant that I no longer like. Even though I didn't like them that particular day, for whatever reason, I can try them anew and perhaps find that I do like them.

I believe that finding a way to make things work is the key. To act as if what I want is a done deal and that I am already successful doing it, is that inner inspiration that needs no approval. It is innocent in a way. It's that innocence of asking an expert out of simple curiosity and admiration, "how did you do that?" Then, as they demonstrate I get it. I make it my own. I become it. I practice it. I share it with others. It's innocent. I believe that as I'm innocently gathering information, doing the next right thing from what I understand at that very moment, learning as much as I can, I need to simply take the next action and see where it takes me.

It's one of these results every time; better, worse, or no change at all. With that, I learn something new. Celebrate it, adjust it, or do it again so as to learn something more. All the while, I stand proudly, confidently, and almost playfully, knowing that it will turn out no matter what.

When the creepy voices in my head start referring to the past, when the whole project crumbles to pieces, when the money runs out for the moment, when the natural disaster takes its toll, as the competitors hack your customer base, when the marketers charge and don't deliver, as the arrogant salon owner hands you your products in a garbage bag, when the buyer tells you how ugly your packaging is, when that family member tells you how stupid everything about you is, when the accountant causes you double taxation, when the factory workers run the wrong recipe, when the web hosting company closes your site for weeks with no explanation, when the supplier overnights a ton of empty bottles with their mistakes to you and leaves you with a bill larger than the cost of a sports car and you now have to pay to have it all recycled and start over....

I remember... that is not me. I am a Platform Artist, I am a musician, I am a manufacturer. I don't have to know how to fix this now.

I simply have to keep on acting like my future is coming true. I am informed by the past. I am defined by the past that shall be called my future and that future is the definition of the true me. On top of that, it can all be kind of really good. Even all the bad stuff? Yes. It's the stuff that makes for a great book, movie or mini-series. Who will I have been once my future has become the past? Now that's something to write about!

Alan Eschenburg, is co-founder of Belegenza, which was developed after a health crisis that ended his platform artist career and almost his hairstyling career altogether. This salon-oriented brand is created of natural ingredients to serve the needs of Alan's private salon customers and his stringent natural health standards. Dedicated to overcoming life's seemingly incessant challenges, Alan stays true to learning from the people in his life, and has attracted elite connections in all areas that span from CEO's to Hollywood's Elite, to top Transformational Educators & elite Beauty and Image Experts.
Website: https://belegenza.com/
Facebook: https://www.facebook.com/AlanGEschenburg

Cheryl Honc

CHAPTER 4
IN SPITE OF IT ALL

It was a warm, balmy, summer night and my cousins called a time out from playing chase to get a drink of water. I remember standing in my uncle's driveway, at six years old, resting on the bumper of his 1981 Chevy truck. Looking in the garage where all of my extended family members were gathered, I witnessed the constant arguing, disrespect, and fighting among them.

It wasn't like this was the first time they argued. It happened practically at all of the family functions. I asked myself, "does this happen in other families"? I didn't have much experience with other people's family gatherings. My parents didn't interact with each other like this. I decided at that moment that this was not how families should treat each other. I realized at that moment that I thought differently than most and felt I didn't belong.

Growing up, I always knew I didn't think the same as the people around me. Most were always a victim of what "the world" did to them. They never considered that they had any responsibility in the matter. They were aware of cause and effect and consequences to one's actions. They didn't feel it applied to them though. I knew they applied to me. I decided I would pay attention to what others did and learn from their mistakes. There was no way I wanted to suffer the way they suffered in learning whatever lesson it was they needed to learn.

Occasionally I wonder if that hindered me. Was I too overly cautious? Should I have gone through with that business transaction? I'd question myself for a moment, and then always conclude that I have taken all of the right actions to get me where I am today. I'll share with you my journey and tie it all up at the end.

I have made and make decisions in my life based on what's the highest good for the people around me, myself, and the future. What action is going to allow us to prosper and increase the flow in cash, business, friends, love, harmony, and relaxation? You probably have heard, whatever you choose to focus on, expands. Focus on prosperity and you get prosperity. Focus on hard work and you get back breaking hard work. You start to find more and more evidence of whatever is your focus.

I regularly visualize what I want the future to hold. I think about it and feel how wonderful it will be when I achieve my goal. I experience the joy, gratification, and excitement of accomplishing my goal; feeling a warm and tingling sensation flow through my body as I experience my accomplishment. Sometimes I do this during a morning run, sipping coffee, or when I need a short break from my daily tasks.

I don't fret on how my future goal is going to happen; I hold for certain that it is going to happen. I clear any limiting beliefs I may have about achieving my goal. Remaining in this state can be a challenge for me at times though. I have people around me that think 97% of everything I do, say, and have is stupid. Occasionally I come across someone that doesn't have my best interests at heart and it is so frustrating. There are times when their negative attitude really affects me. For the longest time, I didn't understand why I was in such an emotional and mental turmoil, until I finally investigated the cause. I discovered that I am highly sensitive to people's feelings, intentions, motivations, and the general energy around them. This is known as being an empath.

Because I feel what's around me, I can suffer from the negative energy. When this happens, I remain positive and repeat positive affirmations to push away the negativity. I remind myself of my future goals and keep taking the next step forward. I remind myself that there is a bigger picture and how so many others will prosper as I prosper.

I eliminate self-negative energy. There's no time for "I can't do it", "I'm tired", or "I don't feel like it". If I were to focus on the negatives, I'm certain I would find plenty of evidence for it to be true. It would just take watching the news for ten minutes. I focus on positive thoughts to have good energy around me so everyone around me can prosper.

Everything I do comes from the perspective of how can I better someone's life. I became a hairstylist to fix all of the bad hair color and haircuts of the world. While standing behind the chair listening to my clients, they confide in me their worries. They've expressed dismay about their hair feeling dry or frizzy or other issue. I've learned from my mentors that I have the best connections in life sitting in my chair. Listening to my clients and their woes in life keeps me listening for solutions to share with them that others may bring to me.

My brother Alan's hands were scarred from working with typical hair products for years every day, all day. As a solution, we created a natural hair care product line called Belegenza.

Our products are made of foods, no chemicals and are safe for humans and the planet. They also address the issues people have with their hair, instead of just masking them temporarily. They are made with premium extracts that penetrate the cortex of the hair to repair and nourish it from the inside out.

We studied cultures around the world for their natural remedies of growing thick, luxurious hair. We took those special ingredients and extracted only the part that benefited the hair and scalp to maximize its benefits. For instance, coconut oil is a large molecule and when applied to hair it will not fully penetrate. It lays on the hair, weighing it down, looking greasy. The hair does receive absorb not receive all of the benefits of coconut oil. When we extract the parts of the coconut oil molecule that can fully penetrate to the cortex of the hair, you maximize its benefits. The hair is moisturized and nourished from the inside, without being weighed down.

This allows us to make extremely concentrated, nutrient-rich formulas. We created Belegenza for ourselves and for everyone to have access to superior hair products that provide results, are natural, affordable, and save the world and ourselves from the typical hair care products full of chemicals.

Surprisingly, clients resisted using our products. They continued to use other inferior products, still complaining about their hair. Some would ask me why their hair looks so good and feels so wonderful when I did it, but not when they did it themselves. I'd tell them it's because of the Belegenza products.

Some continue to resist listening to me and using Belegenza, which feels like the ultimate rejection. Their rejection fells like a kick in the stomach, every time. I finally realized some people are committed more to complaining than finding a solution. Their hair problem was the topic of the day until another problem occurred.

I had clients that struggled with handling their parent's estates when their parent became too ill. Seeing their struggle made me realize that as a society we are not educated properly in the world of finance. I knew the wealthiest people of the world had access to different wealth building tools than a regular person, like me. I just felt that there had to be something out there that would educate and provide wealth tools to the regular person.

One day when my brother and I were on a business trip in California, a long-time friend called him up to reconnect. It so happened she had just moved back to California to the very city we were located. We met up with her later that day for coffee and caught up on each other's lives. She shared with us that she was no longer practicing in mortgage lending. She transitioned into financial services. She was now an agent with World Financial Group (WFG), educating regular people like me, about all the financial tools that the 1% wealthiest of the world already knew. Until WFG, these wealth building tools had not been available to the regular person. No wonder the 1% wealthiest people of the world remained the wealthiest.

She explained how I could put my already taxed money into an investment account and not have to pay taxes on it again when I made interest on it and my principal was guaranteed. Plus it could protect a person if they needed long term care. She was telling me about everything I was looking for, for my clients and other people around me. I was ecstatic!

It felt as if a weight lifted off of me to know that I was going to be able to protect families and their future. I told her WFG is exactly what I needed in my life. She suggested that I become an agent as well so I could start educating those around me and provide all of the tools to protect them financially throughout their life. That's exactly what I did.

I became a WFG financial agent, so everyone around me would have access to the 1% wealthiest wealth building tools. I wanted to make sure that everything someone has worked so hard to accomplish during their life wasn't taken away from them because they didn't learn the rules of the financial and tax game. I wanted to alert them to what is to come with their current financial investment and then show them that they have much better options to choose from.

Sadly, there are some that refuse to listen to me and heed my advice. Again, more rejection. The pain and devastation of rejection from those I care for and want to protect has lessened. I feel that since I have endured so much rejection I have become tolerant of it. I remind myself that I can only contribute to those who feel they need help. Once they do, I'll be there to help. Until then, I listen intently to their problems, hoping to make a difference in their lives.

Another concern I hear a lot about is needing to lose a few pounds. Many are frustrated about needed to drop the last five or so pounds. We're following a healthy diet and exercise program and still can't shed those last pounds.

One summer day Alan and I attended a seminar and noticed that a friend of ours lost a good amount of weight since we had last seen him two months before. He told us he had lost thirty pounds. Alan and I looked at each other and said to him that we needed whatever he was using. Our friend shared that he started drinking a weight loss coffee. Alan and I signed up for it the moment he told us about it. We didn't care if it tasted good or not. It worked that's all that mattered to us. As a bonus, it tastes fantastic!

The coffee is formulated with natural appetite suppressants, feel-good ingredients, and detox components. For optimum performance of the weight loss coffee, it couldn't be accomplished with a single nutrient; it requires a "stack" or group of several independently performing nutrients working together. To deliver this stack of nutrients to the right places in the brain, circulatory support nutrients that promote nitric oxide production and circulation are essential to optimize nutrient potential. Users of this weight loss coffee have experienced little to no sugar cravings, increased energy, increased focus, mental clarity, and decreased appetite. Our friend was like the others we knew, he followed a good diet, exercised and was plateaued at a certain weight. He just needed something to jump start the weight loss. This weight loss coffee was the solution for everyone I knew. How simple, add a cup or two of coffee to your day and watch the weight start pouring off you. Naturally, I became a distributor of this weight loss coffee for those around me that want to lose weight, increase their energy, and their well-being.

Now taking a look at the big picture of what I am creating, it's multiple diversified passive income streams. As a child, when asked what I wanted to do when I grew up, I remember thinking I wanted money to be deposited magically into my bank account automatically as I am enjoying life, vacationing, and shopping. I knew I was going to have to do something until that happened. I wasn't sure what that was though.

I thought about owning a makeup manufacturing facility, owning a business of some kind, being a teacher, flight attendant, computer programmer, or a pharmacist. As I visualized my future, I didn't dwell on the fact that I didn't know how I was going to create my magical deposit of money in my bank account. I just kept taking a step forward, experiencing the present moment, listening to those around me, learning from others' mistakes, sharing with others my goals, seeing where I could contribute to someone else, being open for opportunities to occur, and staying certain of my future.

Along this journey, I have suffered emotional turmoil from people's negative energy and being told that everything I did was stupid. At times I even considered that they were correct. I'd wallow in self-doubt while eating junk food and binge-watching television. Eventually, I'd snap out of it and push the negative self-talk away.

How could protecting a person's health, well-being, and financial security be a bad idea? My creation allows for anyone to participate in any way they wish. Their hair and well-being are taken care of with Belegenza's food grade products. Their assets are financially secure for the future and in case of a catastrophic event. Their body and mind are nourished with the functional weight loss coffee.

Not only do all of these things protect them, but it also provides an opportunity for anyone else to provide the same things to the people they love and create their passive income streams. They can build it as big or as small as their heart desires. They too have access to having money deposited magically in their bank account as they are out enjoying life, vacationing, and shopping.

I wake up every morning knowing that I'm going to have an extraordinary amount of resistance from others, so I follow the system I've created for myself in order to keep going in spite of it all. For all of those that think everything I do is stupid; if these are my stupid ideas, then I look forward to my amazing ideas!

Cheryl Honc, co-founder of Belegenza, the world's finest and first luxury silicone-free beauty care line, also owns several profitable businesses that help with weight loss, hair growth without chemicals, access to risk free money building tools by the top 1% wealthiest in the world, and access to celebrities top business mentors trainings. Cheryl takes the complex and simplifies it in a way that is easily integrated. Her guidance is life-changing as she shows you how to arrange every action you take into one that serves your life and passion.

Email: cheryl@belegenza.com
Hair care: www.belegenza.com
Weight loss coffee: www.thepowercoffee.com
Wealth building: www.yourwealthbuilding.com

Carmen Ventrucci

CHAPTER 5
AUTHENTICITY DESIGNED MY LIFE

If you would have told me when I was in high school that I would have six kids, I would have laughed at you and used creative language to tell you that I would never have that many children. With my drive and ambition, I felt destined for something better than "just motherhood," especially motherhood in that quantity. I was executive material. I was going to work for a large corporation and make a difference. I couldn't tell you what that difference was then, I'd figure it out later.

Well, guess what, I have six children. Four of our own and two nieces that I raise with my husband. Funny how "I will never" turned into "bring it on!"

Now coming up on my 20-year high school reunion, I'm the same person. I have the same drive, same ambition, and I'm making a difference. Now I know what that difference is. Part of my identity is being a mom, a badass mom to be exact. Although I didn't foresee it in high school, I am proud to be a badass mom and I wouldn't trade it for the world.

Here's the part that makes me a badass, I avoid looking for perfection and embrace who I am, allowing my authenticity to inspire those around me to prosperity and to design the lives they want to lead.

Six months ago I had a revelation, a surreal moment. I was sitting alone in my dark living room with only the light of the Christmas tree. I was listening to my friend speak on a video. He said that he had really taken the time to stop, embrace his authenticity, and live the life that he designed instead of living one that was designed for him. When I heard those words, I burst into tears. What he said struck me with so much force, because I realized that was not how I was living my life. I was living the life that others gave me. It only took me a second to realize that I had an illusion of control. I was not spending my time doing what I truly wanted to do. I was a master at dealing with what emerged, I was so busy playing defense I forgot to go on offense and design the life I want to live. I was too busy being busy that I was losing sight of the important things. I had trouble remembering the last quality time I had with my kids and husband. The last date night we had was three months ago. What the hell was I doing? Where did all my time go, and how was it already Christmas?

This was a turning point for me. It took crying in a dark room by the Christmas tree for me to realize that I had to take action and make changes, so I could be the most authentic person and live my definition of a prosperous life.

I decided to take account of how I was spending my time. I knew in order to be prosperous I had to spend time on prosperity creating activities and not the "busy work" that is normally associated with raising six kids, being a wife, and having a career. Surprisingly, or not surprisingly, I was spending time on the wrong things. Activities that made me who I am were taking a backseat to other random bullshit in my day. Physical activity, reading books, exploring new recipes, quality time with the kids, helping others build plans to achieve their dreams, that is who I am. Doing laundry, falling asleep on the couch in front of the TV, that is what I was doing. (I remedied some of that by having my oldest start a company and I hire her to do the laundry. She gets to learn accountability and basic business skills in a safe environment and earn a few bucks, I get my time. Win-win.)

That is a perfect example of when I'm authentic. I love making deals and negotiating. Thinking creatively, outside the box, is when I prosper. Finding those win-win situations, those Nash Equilibriums (a game theory in business strategy), is what I do best.

My education and upbringing groomed me for Corporate America and it was a waste. That is not how I think. It took me a long time to realize and accept that. Now, instead of measuring my success by the next promotion, I use a different set of metrics, my own. Success means that I have my independence. Success means that I answer to me and the ones I really care about. Success means that I am an inspiration for others around me. It means I can make people laugh; it means I can make them smile. Above all, success means I am teaching my kids to be authentic so they can find their prosperity.

I am grateful for my experience in Corporate America. I was provided a wealth of knowledge on individualization, how to handle certain people in certain situations, which has served me well in all aspects of life. Because I spent sixteen years there, I know now I am meant to be someplace else.

So, stop. What is your definition of prosperity for you? Not your family's definition, not your job's definition, not society's definition, yours. The path to authenticity starts within; first you must be yourself and be true to yourself to be authentic to others.

Authenticity is what gives us courage to stand up, face our fears, and be who we truly are. When we understand how we are best authentic we are unstoppable. Authenticity has many other names like truth, genuineness, fearlessness, and courage. Acting as our authentic self, empowers us and others to communicate more clearly, be bold, go for what we want, and prosper in all areas of life.

Reflect on your authenticity and how it helps you prosper. Everyone's journey is different, here is how I approached mine.

<u>Know who you are, then embrace it.</u> Self-reflection is not easy for everyone. Fortunately, there are plenty of personality assessments out there that can help you figure out who you are. Think of your personality as a system. With any system there are always loopholes and ways to game it. Figure out your strengths and use them. Likewise, with your weaknesses. Game your "personality system" for the way you learn to become faster, better, smarter, and unleash your authentic self. For example, one of my strengths is that I'm an achiever, I have the capability to get things done. To capitalize on this and make sure I'm focusing my energy on the most important things, I make a list every day of the seven things I need to accomplish that day and plan to complete them by noon. This helps me accomplish the most important things for that day and plays to my strength of an achiever.

While you're doing your self-reflection write down your core values, your fundamental beliefs, and the foundation on which you conduct yourself. These are the things most important to you that when out of alignment, need to get back on track for you to function. I have seven, mine are: Family, health, intelligence, independence, clarity, humor, and authenticity. Every day I ask myself if I was aligned with my core values. "Did I laugh today? Was I healthy? Did I tell my family I love them? Was I authentic?" Answering yes means I'm on track, no means I have to make adjustments and course corrections. I don't bat

100%, however my average has improved since I started this exercise.

<u>Know what you want.</u> Whether it's a personal, professional, or a relationship-based goal, know what you want. This is the most basic way to be authentic because if you know what you want, you take action towards that goal. Remember the phrase, actions speak louder than words? Pay attention to your actions. Are they leading you in the right direction? What do your daily tasks say about what you want? What does your procrastination say about what you want?

Right now, I have a plan to become a black belt in Taekwondo in the year 2020. Why? Because it aligns with my core values of health, intelligence, and family (seven of the eight people in my house participate and it's really fun to kick people) and I have milestones set to measure my success along my path. Right now, that is my definition of success in that area of my life and I consider myself prosperous for working towards and achieving that plan.

If you are still figuring out what you want, that's okay, be honest with yourself and admit that. Set time aside to think and define your plan. Experiment and try new things to find out what you do want, it's okay to change course. If something does not work out you are not a failure, you just found a way that didn't work.

<u>Embrace mistakes, it's how we learn</u>. I constantly remind my kids of this. If they get a nine out of ten right on a spelling test, I guarantee they will remember how to spell that one word they missed. Many of us were raised to be ashamed of our mistakes, believing that perfection is the goal. I disagree completely. I make mistakes every day and plan to continue making mistakes every day for the rest of my life.

With some mistakes comes the art of the apology. I admit it took me awhile to master this, let's face it, it's not easy or fun for many. However, sometimes a sincere apology is just what is needed to remedy a situation and move on towards prosperity. And remember, never follow an apology with an excuse, that's not really an apology.

Manage your priorities. I personally think time management is crap. Time is finite for all of us and we'll only get so much time, so managing it is a losing battle. I often see the concept of time management leading people into the "too busy being busy" mentality that doesn't lead to efficiency, achievement, or quality production (this is especially true for parents). Instead, I believe in managing your priorities. Priority management is the key to authenticity and prosperity, because it is about maximizing the time we have. If it's important to me, I do it. If it's not, I don't. Simple. I learned how to say no to, or outsource things that are outside the alignment of who I am.

More importantly, I learned to say yes to the things that are inside the alignment of who I am. Be bold, say yes to what is important to you. Apply for that job even though you might only meet 75% of the qualifications. Go to that pottery class you want to take, because you've always been curious. If it's scary its usually worth it. I said yet to writing this chapter for this book. I wasn't sure what words would pour out of me, yet I knew I had to do it. I knew if I said yes, I would figure it out.

Priority management also extends to my kids and husband. If something is their priority, it becomes mine. I might despise a sport or their favorite activity, yet if it becomes their passion, I am behind them 100%.

Find your village, the network of people that will support you through life's joys, trials, and tribulations. We often hear the expression, "it takes a village to raise a child," and while this is true (take it from this mama) it is so much more than that. It takes a village to do almost anything: create processes, run a business, develop personally, complete projects, and create great leaders. I don't care who you are, or how good you think you are, you cannot do everything by yourself, you need the support of your village. Your village will look different from your neighbors due to your specific needs and objectives. Building it is one of the absolutely most important steps you must take to be prosperous. It took me awhile to realize and accept this lesson because I wanted to do it on my own, I wanted to be in control of my destiny. Now, I realize building a village and network is a tool, it's a resource that gives you more control of the destiny you desire to create.

Our network of relationships shows us who we really are. People join the village of those they trust, authentic individuals who truly care about others and their families. Building a network, or village, is about capitalizing on the greatness in you to bring out the greatness in others to accomplish extraordinary things.

Showing vulnerability quickly builds rapport and building rapport allows us to quickly bring people into our village. Vulnerability lets us build relationships rapidly and at a much more meaningful level because it reveals our authentic self. Part of my journey to authenticity was learning to share my vulnerabilities. I admit, I felt horrified about this concept. Then I found its power. People connect with imperfections, not perfection and figuring out how to tactfully share my vulnerabilities helped me gain rapport with others much faster. In fact, rapport became almost instant once I started doing this.

The next time someone asks you, "How are you?" notice how you answer. Chances are you say, "Fine," or, "Good." Instead try this. Answer, "I'm awesome. I'm having a challenge getting a meeting with this particular person. Do you happen to know them?" This is the perfect opportunity to start a conversation and build rapport. Use this format for whatever challenge you're facing, whether it be personal or professional. It shows you're working towards a goal and allows people to help. Usually, people genuinely want to help. If you must give a one-word answer, use awesome, perfect, or fantastic; it's more interesting than "good."

My network, my village, is wide and deep. It's comprised of men, women, and children who are millionaires, laborers, professionals, business owners, parents, singles, and everything in between. My network has delivered for me countless times, that is something I do not take for granted. They have helped me prosper in many ways from doing business deals, to taking fun vacations, to caring for my family, even informing me of the opportunity to contribute to this book. When we took in our nieces a year ago, my hockey team got together and brought us a car-full of food to help with welcoming them and with the uptick in the grocery bill. I was, and am, so grateful for their generosity and care because it helped us prosper as a family unit. My village responds when I ask them to, because I treat them with respect and I show up for them when they need me.

<u>Be the village.</u> You have to show up for your network and relationships in a way that is genuine and meaningful for you. A network is like a tissue, a living organism that requires nourishment and sustenance. Some help others by giving time, others by giving money, or their talents. Me, I'm a connector, I have a knack for knowing a guy that knows a guy, and am frequently making networking connections for my friends. I'm also a great listener. Friends and colleagues often seek me for advice on everything from parenting to finances to personal development.

Being the village can be simple. If you read an article that makes you think of someone, email it to them. Wish people happy birthday on their favorite social media platform. Little gestures that show others you're keeping them in your orbit go a long way in maintaining rapport in your village. When people know that you care about them as a human being, they will be motivated to help you.

Celebrate and have fun; if we're not having fun, then what's the point? There are so many reasons to be grateful in this life that you must take time to celebrate and acknowledge even the little things. I'm not talking about participation awards where you get a trophy just for showing up. I'm talking about keeping things in perspective and expressing true gratitude for the everyday miracles we experience and sometimes don't even notice. So set milestones, find joy in the journey, and be sure there is plenty of fun and laughter in the life you design.

My journey to find and acknowledge my authenticity was a turning point in my life. It allowed me to face fears, design my life, appreciate my village, and have more fun.

Embrace your badass and design your life, find your village, be the village.

Carmen Ventrucci is a self-described "Badass Mom" to 4 of her own children and 2 of her nieces. Carmen is a master at using mindset, process, and continuous improvement to create financial and personal success. She believes that boldness is rewarded and lives this belief to the fullest; she recently left Corporate America and founded her own company, True Sisu Life. Carmen is an avid hockey player who also enjoys doing and learning new things. Her newest obsession is taekwondo, she currently has her red belt and is progressing towards a black belt.
Carmen is available for private consultations.
Email: carmen@truesisulife.com
Website: TrueSisuLife.com

Lisa Manzo

CHAPTER 6
JOURNEY OF CHANGE

Talent alone won't make you a success. Neither will being in the right place at the right time, unless you are ready. The most important question is, 'Are you ready? Johnny Carson

I was just existing. Struggling to make ends meet and enjoy life. I was depressed, frustrated, discouraged, and lonely; to name a few of my feelings. This had been going on for a long time. Change needed to occur. I wanted to press the reset button and start over. I decided to move to North Carolina and do just that. I started with two goals in mind. First, to lose weight. Second, to give up alcohol. And as the saying goes, "We plan, and God laughs!" I say this because there was no straight route to the destination. The destination had its ups and downs. I had my struggles. The most important part is **the journey began.**

I took a long hard look at my life and figured out I was not going where I wanted. I had no dreams, no goals, and no ambition. I had been trying to change things through the years. At forty I got my teaching license. At fifty I got my nursing license. While both these professions are wonderful, I didn't feel that either was what I was put on the planet to accomplish. I figured the move would help me find my way. I didn't realize how long this journey would take. I'm glad I started, otherwise I would be in that old state of mind.

This journey started around 2007. My daughter was a Freshman in high school and my son was in middle school. I wanted to pick up and leave New York with my children. We discussed this as a family and both of my kids agreed to go. The only challenge was the radius clause in my divorce agreement, which stated I could only move a certain number of miles from where we were living. North Carolina was not within that distance so I asked my former husband about moving. He thought about and said, "No." I understood that. If I was in his position I would have said no as well. Now here is the part that gets to me, four months later he picks up and moves to Florida. I would never move my children in the middle of a school year unless there were no other options. So, I waited and near the end of the school year my children and I discussed it again. At that point daughter didn't want to move. So, we stayed.

During this time, I distanced myself from some of my friends because I felt I was the one who was keeping these friendships alive. I was putting in all the work and it felt one sided. I came to the realization that if my "friends" didn't value me enough to make an effort, they were not really friends (remember this thought, as we will come back to it). I want to be with people who value me and whom I value. I was also in a long-term relationship that was not going in the direction I wanted it to go. We weren't a team. We no longer supported each other and couldn't find the way back.

Going back to the planning and God laughing; it is now ten years later and I'm planning to move on February 9, 2017. Ha-ha, that doesn't happen. We get ten inches of snow and I move the next day.

Let's discuss weight. It first became an issue for me when I realized as a child that my weight was something that I could control. This is important to understand because I felt I had no control over what was happening in my life. For example, when I was eight-years old I was going to make my communion and I made the mistake of complimenting my mom on her beehive hair style. My aunt happened to be there at the time and together they decided that I would have that hair style for my communion. Even at eight years old I knew there was nothing I could say that would stop this from happening. Remember, I came from the generation where most adults believed that children should be seen and not heard. My opinion and my thoughts didn't matter. My solution to the problem in my eight-year old mind was to cut my hair so it wouldn't be long enough.

I went in my room and took out my pair of kid's scissors and started cutting. I remember it being difficult to do, but I was very determined. I must have been in there a long time because my mom came to see what I was doing. When she entered my room and saw what I was up to she yelled at me for a while. I don't know what how long it actually was. But in my eight-year old mind It felt like forever and that it was never going to end. Then my mom kept asking. "Why would you do that?" I was thinking that I was so happy because now they couldn't give me that dumb hairstyle. The voice in my head kept repeating, "At least I don't have to wear that hair style."

Of course, I was wrong and with the hair I did have left my aunt did her best to bestow on me that beehive style. Ugh! Even when I tried to get control, it didn't work.

When I was twelve years old, I realized that my weight was something I could control. I think this was my way of calling out for help. I wanted to be heard. I have been experiencing the ups and downs of weight gain and weight loss ever since.

Fast forward to February 2017, when I joined a weight loss program again because when I follow that plan it works. I begin to lose weight, which is a good thing. I did lose weight and I was making progress and feeling better about myself. It took me eleven months and I lost fifteen pounds. I must have been really determined as I was binge drinking alcohol and not exercising.

I was in North Carolina for a few months, when I realized being there was a step backwards and not a step forward as I had thought it would be. Financially I was worse off than when I was in New York. I was short even more money for my bills and I had to get a second job. If I had done my proper due diligence, I would have figured this out before I moved. I couldn't go anywhere or do anything because I had no money. Boy, did that sound familiar. I had been living like this for the last twenty years and it needed to change.

I googled "free things to do in Durham, NC" and found a two-hour seminar about real estate. Thinking that was something I would like to learn about, I went. I was intrigued and signed up for the 3-day weekend event. At that event I had the vision that this is going to be life changing for me and I signed up for real estate investment education. Now I knew I had to get out of my own head. I needed to educate myself and change my thought patterns. I started listening to audio books and joining entrepreneur groups. I was determined to change my life no matter what.

In January of 2018 I was at my first boot camp (aka 3-day educational event) for real estate investing. There was a fitness challenge being offered and I thought to myself, *I need this. I can stop being a couch potato.* I asked no questions (not something I recommend) and signed up. I'm thinking *This is great. It's a 60-day challenge and there is no way I'm going to an event with 200+ people and fail.*

This is how the plan works. They send you the workouts and you do them at your level of fitness. Mind you I could not do all the exercises. For example, I did 3 burpees when I started and thought my heart was going to explode. I held off on the burpees until I got in better shape and lost more weight. I made a chart, to track my weekly weight and monthly measurements. I also took a starting picture and a few more pictures along the way. The mind is funny, and you forget things so easily and I needed to be reminded that I was making progress. I could feel the change in my body as I was losing weight, so I needed to see it on a chart as validation that my hard work is paying off.

For the challenge we had a private Facebook group to help motivate each other and celebrate our successes. In addition, we also had weekly calls for motivation. Early on I was seeing great success because I had been a couch potato for so long. I was about five weeks in and had already lost six inches off my waist. I was so glad I measured. It was good to know that I was succeeding at this. I received a shout out on one of the calls from one of the moderators of the group and my momentum increased.

The fitness event itself was wonderful and there were some amazing speakers. The biggest impact on me was when the members were able to talk about their emotional struggles. We got to hear from the attendees in addition to the speakers. Lisa at the camp talked about how she was not encouraged by her family and didn't have their support. Her sharing was very emotional for me as I could feel her pain. It was great hearing someone else speak who felt like me and had the resolve to overcome her experiences. Now I was thinking *if she can do it so can I. Let's go home and ride the momentum!* I got home, joined the gym and continued to make progress. I wasn't in a hurry to lose the weight because I believe it should come off the way you put it on; over time. If I was making progress, all was good. No matter how small, progress is progress.

Now let's go to the alcohol. I had known for a while

that I needed to stop consuming alcohol. I was a binge drinker, who drank after work. Drinking has its own compartment in my brain. For me, that means I can have one and walk away. When I have two, I don't walk away. I drink until I pass out. It had to stop. I was not living.

For a long time, I thought drinking did not interfere with my life. For example, I did a two-year nursing program in ten months. I was wrong. Time was moving and my drinking was getting worse. I was realizing that the drinking was making me lazy. I would drink and then the next day I had no energy, no motivation, and no desires. I was a lump on the couch watching TV. My life was passing by and I was not participating in things that brought me joy. Clearly my thinking was incorrect. Alcohol was interfering with my life. Remember my previous thought about my friendships being one sided? Since I stopped drinking, I have figured out that people didn't want to be around me because of the alcohol. That was eye opening and painful for me to admit. I had to admit to myself that it was me and not them.

It had now been about a year that I had been thinking about and asking for help (in my head) to stop drinking. It was March 2018 and I decided to pay for a medium reading over the phone. My dad passed in 2015 and enough time has passed that I wanted to hear what the medium had to say. The medium establishes early in the call that I need to let him talk and not tell him who I want to speak with. It was a 45-minute call. About 20 minutes in, he figures out that he is connecting with my dad. Then he said to me something to the effect of, "I don't know why I am telling you this or what it means. Your dad wants you to know when you get those thoughts when you are driving in the car to pull over and ask for help." He asks me if I understand. I most certainly do understand. So, let me explain it to you.

I live in North Carolina and unlike where I lived in New York, there are liquors stores everywhere. The closest liquor store is about four miles from my house. On my way home from work I would think, *Should I get a bottle, or shouldn't I?* So, I would drive to the liquor store and know I really shouldn't get the bottle and then drive home. I would get home and decide I should get a bottle, then drive back to the liquor store. When I got to the liquor store I'd decide I shouldn't get a bottle. Sometimes I'd drive to the store and buy a bottle on the first time. Other times I'd drive back and forth from my house to the liquor store for an hour. Sometimes I would win, but most times I lost the battle and I bought a bottle. This was a vicious cycle. Now I have won the war!

After the phone call I dumped the remaining vodka down the drain and I haven't had a drink since. I still had those thoughts, especially on the way home from work. The interesting part of the this is that the thoughts got less and less and when I did think about it, I would ask for help and it would be given. Either I would remember something I had to do and focus on that or my phone would ring, and I would get distracted. I fully believed that help would be provided, and it was.

Anger was a huge trigger for me. I would get angry and not want to feel that way. I didn't want to feel my feelings. So, I drank. Now when I get angry, I go to a quiet place by myself and analyze why I am angry and does it have any merit, or I meditate, or go for a walk. I figure out a way to resolve the situation without alcohol. Acknowledging my feelings and working through the emotions work best. It is also very hard to do. I have chosen now to respond instead of reacting. If something generates a strong emotional feeling, I walk away and think or meditate about it. This helps me to figure things out. I put a name to the emotion I am feeling. After giving my emotion a name, I can usually figure out the reasoning behind my feelings and deal with them.

Drinking does not resolve the issue. The feelings are still there when you are sober. Therapy is also helpful.

Remember you have friends and it's okay to ask your friends for help. Asking for help is something I have always struggled with. I am getting better at it. Your friends are on call at the moment in time when you are struggling. In order to see my therapist I have to wait for an appointment and sometimes things can't wait.

The first forty-five days were the hardest. I thought about alcohol every day. Then thinking about drinking came less often. As time went on, my thoughts about alcohol decreased in frequency.

Then for the next challenge. I was at a networking event in Cancun. All you can drink included in the price. *How am I going to get through this week?* First, I made a friend who doesn't like to drink and I spent a lot of time with her. This was part of the help that was given, because I asked from a good place in my heart and not out of desperation. I was wandering the hotel looking for something to do and I passed the bar. I knew I couldn't sit at the bar because it would be too tempting. So I saw some people I know sitting in the back, not at the bar. I went in and picked my seat very carefully, in the back away from the bar.

I was looking at the view outside the hotel instead of the bar, so alcohol was not in my line of sight. I was networking and the server came over and I ordered an iced tea. Bob told the server to put some alcohol in the drink. I explain to Bob that I am sober for 75 days and drinking is not on my agenda. This was the first time I admitted to someone who didn't know me that I was an alcoholic. I had no emotional response to this. It was as if I had released this demon from my head when I acknowledged the alcoholism. Then Bob congratulated me for coming to the event and not drinking. I didn't realize what an accomplishment this was at the time. Reflecting on it I realize how powerful that moment was when I chose not to drink and I acknowledged my problem.

Originally, I was going to have a drink on my 1-year

anniversary. I have since realized that was the alcoholic in my brain knocking on the door. I realized this because I have also given up soda. Every once in a while, I will have a soda. The thing is, it is never only one. I drink four or five of them in a row or I go to gas station and get the largest size and drink it and still want more. I then applied that logic to the alcohol and realized alcohol will be the same. I'm not opening the door and I did not drink on the anniversary! That door needs to stay bolted forever.

I have since started a journal about my victories. When I'm feeling negative emotions, I get out my book and read about all my successes and it changes the way I feel. During the journey I have come to realize that I was listening to what other people thought I should be or do. I came to the conclusion that it was time to be authentic and do what I am passionate about.

When I started this journey of change, I didn't realize what I was doing was, "Daring to Authentic." I didn't know it had a name. I feel that I am getting comfortable in my own skin. I have lost forty-six pounds and I have reached my 1-year alcohol free anniversary! In my mind I have already ended the ups and downs of weight and alcohol. I am going to get to my goal weight and stay there. I am going to remain alcohol free. Life is good! I am enjoying the journey even when it is hard. When I look back, I feel good about where I am now and the journey doesn't seem as difficult as it was when I started.

My journey continues and the next step is to be a coach and help other people in their journeys. So as Johnny Carson says, "...Are you ready?" We can start your journey together.

Lisa Manzo is a Life Coach helping kickstart new lifestyles. She can be contacted at:
Email: LisaManzo.LM@gmail.com
Phone: 914-980-1593
Website: www.theLisaManzo.com

Cesar R. Espino

CHAPTER 7
OVERCOMING ADVERSITY

Every person in this world has the same potential to become the very best version of themselves, regardless of the family they were born into. The major challenge is that some of us look at the world, the circumstance, the challenge with a different type of lens and that view or perspective can impact how we live our lives.

Understanding today's society, I realized that in order for my life to change I had to change my own lens, to give myself the opportunity to see the world differently and work on a particular life purpose. This however did not come easy or without any major struggles. For me the life challenge and struggle began in January 27, 1980, the day I was born to a single mother and in a developing country. Not only was I born to one parent, (to this point I have no clue who my biological father is, nor do I know his name or even care). I was also born into a family of the lowest Mexican Social Hierarchy. Mexico classifies its citizens into particular groups, so this meant that by not being part of a higher classification, there were challenges or struggles that my family had to face. They had the option to accept things as they were, or make the shifts in life to improve the situation called life.

Before I can share with you the changes that I made in order to change the lens in my life, I want to illustrate for you where I came from and how I got to the present moment. First and foremost, I want you to see my life story as a lesson, an inspiration, and a blue print of never giving up. I believe that *You Can Overcome Anything! Even When the World Says "No"*. As you read my story, I want to empower you to NOT accept what may seem as the only options offered by society, current situations, and life challenges. Overcoming those obstacles by being certain, focused, and having the right mindset will gear your life to abundance.

A failure is a lesson, a lesson is a reward, a reward is the opportunity to an abundant life. - Cesar R. Espino

Growing up as a kid in Mexico City was not what I would consider to be a normal childhood. A normal kid, regardless of their poverty level, has the opportunity to play afterschool, possibly have a birthday celebration every year, and live day by day only worrying about being a kid and letting the days or years just pass. Unfortunately, or perhaps as I realized later in life "fortunately", I was not a normal kid, since my family and I were so poor we had to improvise to survive. To begin with, my family was so poor that we lived in a 200 square feet room that had no running water inside, no insulation, was made out of sheet metal and plywood, and had no flooring. The house sat right on top of pure dirt, (we lived and slept directly on top of dirt). This room, which we did not own, was what we called home and where four of us (my mom, grandma, older brother, and I) lived. During this time the real challenge was not our living conditions. Although they were not ideal, the real challenge was that in my early childhood I was faced with two major obstacles that forced me to grow up right away.

First, at just four years old, my mom decided to take a chance at life by making the decision to leave me and my family (grandma and older brother) behind, as she made her way to the American dream and migrated to the US. As a kid I was confused because I did not comprehend how my mom could do this to me. How could she leave me behind, not knowing why nor when I would see her again? That was painful especially at my early age. Her leaving us behind forced me to have my second challenge in my short period of life and from this point forward my childhood life changed forever.

Because of our financial situation, I had to become a man rather quickly and leave behind the life of a child. My grandma was a firm believer in education and therefore I had to go to school every day. After school, in order for us to survive and to put food on the table, we had to work to make money. Also, there were many times throughout my first ten years when all we had to eat was the Mexican specially dish, tortillas with some grains of salt.

After I got home from school, I worked by helping my family prepare and stir flour, knead, and roll dough We created different types of cookie shapes (like stars), baked them, and got them ready for sale. We also baked bread. We sold them near my elementary school at a *tianguis* (flea market). This was hard because many times the amount of money made was much lower than the money spent to bake the bread and cookies. This forced us to come up with additional product offerings and soon after we began to also offer quesadillas, taquitos, and *obleas* (wafers). Not only did I have to work hard to survive, I also learned to live my life without my mom and for a second even forgot about her as I felt all alone in this world. All I could see was the three of us, (my grandma, older brother, and I), struggling, working, and surviving in a corrupt society.

It is sad to know that there are many countries where the society forces its citizens to start working at an early age just to be able to survive. This was my reality as a kid and for most of my early childhood. My life was just going to school, coming home, and working. I did not have time to play with other kids on the block or go to a friend's house. As a matter of fact, if I was not working, we were not generating the income needed to help us live.

Finally, once we were able to save some money, both from what we earned and from the money my mom saved while being in the US, we had enough to build a similar house to the one we lived in, except this time on our own land. This was also not an easy process, as my grandma had to send a letter to the city delegate, not asking rather pleading, to allow us to build a house in a land that was left behind to her by my grandpa who I'd never met. After many months of going through this process, the city delegate granted us the ability to build and for once we had something that we could call our own home. The living conditions were similar to our rental home, yet it was sufficient and fulfilling as this was our own and any money saved would help us construct a better home.

In 1987, three years after my mom left, the unexpected finally happened. My grandma mentioned that we would be traveling to the US to visit my mom. This was a bitter sweet moment, as I still was confused as to why she had left me in the first place. Nevertheless, we had the opportunity to travel to the US and this trip was surreal. Before I knew it, I was making my way to Tijuana Mexico to cross into the US via the Southern US border. The challenge we faced t was that we had no legal documentation, the same reason why my mom did not come to Mexico and instead had us travel on our own to Tijuana.

At that time, my mom paid approximately $500 per person to have us cross over the border with a *coyote* (human smuggler). I still remember this experience as if it was yesterday. We crossed through the mountains and due to helicopter patrolling we had to hide and duck in the bushes, very much like what you see in some movies. That was not the only thing, we had to walk for what seemed to be an eternity and because of my age, height, and not being able to swim, when we arrived at a river, I had to be carried to cross over. The water was cold, it was dark, and it was the middle of the night. Because of heavy patrols we had to stay overnight at a place before the second check point. The following day we were united with my mom and for the first time I met the person who at that time I did not see as my father, but has now recognized me as his kid and I am proud to call father.

It was official, for the first time in my life I was in a different country where I actually had new clothes, new shoes, plenty of food to eat, and where I did not have to worry about working to survive. It felt great because I was living the life that I had never imagined for me and my mom made sure that we enjoyed our time in the US. She even purchased matching clothes for my brother and me as if we were twins. Every theme park we went to we wore matching clothes.

Since living the US, I have never met anyone that has gone to every single theme park in Southern California as we did in our first visit to the US. The sad part is that this was a dream, because I was just a visitor and my time here ended rather quickly and as fast as I made my way to the US, I found myself packing to go back to Mexico, to my true reality.

This was another thing I did not understand; we went through all that trouble to cross the border and yet we couldn't stay. Before I knew it we were back to our old life, and I found myself again working and having that life I was born into. This time around, we were not baking or selling in the *tianguis*, we were actually sewing clothes for dolls. At just seven years old I had my own sewing machine, and I've learned and still to this day know how to sew clothes. For the next couple of years things were mostly the same.

Then God gave me a second chance at life. Because we still lived in a house made out of sheet metal and plywood, the nights got pretty cold. On one occasion, I came down with a chronic cold and typhoid fever. Not having the financial means, my grandma attempted to treat my illness with household remedies, which did nothing for me. The day she decided to take me to *La Cruz Roja*, the Dr. was very upset with my grandma. He told her that if she would have waited one more day, she would have been burying me rather than saving me. I was submerged in an ice-cold shower to bring down the high fever and was given medicine and treatment. This was for sure a scare and today I've realized that this was a chance to make an impact not only in my life and but in the life of others.

The year 1990 is a year to remember for me, because this is the year that we found ourselves making our way back to the US. Although I did not know whether or not to believe if this was real or was just another teaser like the previous time. All I knew was I would be making my way back to the states. I also knew this was my mom's way of giving me a better life and taking me out of the poverty and a corrupted society I had always lived in.

It turned out to be a permanent move and I saw this as my next big challenge in life. Although it was very difficult to overcome, I am glad I did not allow the negative influences, the unknown, and the fear to get the best of me. First, I was a stranger in this new country. I had no friends and I was not able to communicate since I knew not one word in English. Because of this I was humiliated to the point that I begged my mom to send me back to Mexico, to what looked normal and familiar to me, regardless of my many struggles.

Thank God she did not listen to me, because that was the easy way out and I would have been running away from the unknown. Instead I made a choice, changed my lens and decided to educate myself, to fit in, and to surpass above and beyond what I thought was possible. In just two years of being in the US, I was able to communicate fluently in English and further became a straight "A" student, graduated with honors from middle school, and even had the pleasure to address the graduating class by delivering a speech to them called We Choose Our Way.

I stayed away from gangs, tagging crews, and the negative influences, which were many during my middle and high school years. One thing to consider is that no matter how hard it may seem and no matter what life puts in front of you, you must face it head on and deal with what emerges. I had similar success in my high school years with only one exception. At the age of 16 I had to once again grow up pretty fast as I had as a kid This however did not stop me and made me have an even higher purpose to succeed.

Today's failures and setbacks are tomorrow's rewards, deal with what emerges and keep pushing forward! -Cesar R. Espino

Once I became an adult and I started my professional career, I was stable and had much success with my education and career. I held multiple jobs in management and with worldwide companies and at the same time earned several degrees including my MBA. At one point in my life I felt I was on top of the world and thought that there was nothing else for me to do as I continued to work with top tier companies. I felt I was set for the rest of my life. Yet, once again I had to focus my lens and realized that I was not quite done. I had many setbacks, failures, and many mistakes that broke me down. However, I knew I had much more to give and this was not the end for me.

I am not perfect and I've been handed down so many lessons except I've learned, I've grown, and the rest of my life I will live becoming the best version of me each and every day. - Cesar R. Espino

Having decided to invest in the rest of my life and to go through what I consider my transformation phase, I had to make several changes which I encourage any person to do in their own life to reach greatness. By now I have realized that seeking for more and searching for my true journey is not an easy path to take. Yet, when I badly want it, I have to fight for it. No matter who gets in my way or who tells me that I can't or what life throws at me, if it is my desire to seek greatness, it is my responsibility to never give up.

Making large breakthroughs take time and start with small changes and mind shifts. - Cesar R. Espino

The changes I had to make in my personal life came down to attending non-traditional schooling and learning about finances, businesses, and entrepreneurship through seminars. I've made several investments and have joined masterminds, inner circle communities, and have gotten into mentorship programs. Just as importantly I changed other principles and priorities by doing the following;

I decided to get rid of any negative programming, for example, the news, watching TV shows, movies or any other content on TV that is not helping me improve my current situation.

I decided to let go of listening to radio stations while driving. Instead I listen to motivational videos, eBooks (enhancing my thoughts, providing ideas to improve my life and business).

I put into practice each and every day the life savers found in The Miracle Morning: silence, meditation, prayer, affirmations, visualization, exercise, reading, journaling.

I read out loud affirmations twice a day, every day (influenced by The Secret and Think and Grow Rich).

I created two visions boars (influenced by The Secret and The Miracle Morning).

I read daily to improve my programming and thinking.

I found and got involved with a local church group to get more spiritually focused.

I attend self-development and business development seminars as often as possible such as The Turning Point by Marshall Sylver.

To continue to improve my or even your own personal and professional life, these are the basic drivers that must be adopted. Just as important as it is to have a healthy diet, it is important to have the right programming and mind triggers. Additionally, I must create disciplines or rituals to assist in all areas of improvement, for example affirmations as the right type of programming. The next thing to consider is physiology, when the mind is aligned with the physiology and creates an action as if what is desired is real. Then, what is seen in mind and the way it is acted in real life will eventually become one of the same. Lastly, I focus on continuous non-traditional education to further expand my knowledge such as; masterminds, inner circle communities, mentors, and being part of networking groups.

Be grateful, appreciate life, connect with a power greater than you, and have faith that no one and nothing can stop you from reaching your set plans.

I will do what it takes to make it happen before dying! And I will not die not doing what it takes to make it happen! - Cesar R. Espino

Cesar R. Espino was born in Mexico City to a single mom and into a poor family. He started working at the tender age of five in a society of poverty and what seemed a future with no hope. From this point forward Cesar had to adjust to life and create his own path. It took numerous challenges and changes in life to create what is now a successful and promising future. He now holds a master's degree, is an entrepreneur with several businesses, and encourages others to follow their dreams regardless of their circumstances.
Email: C2realestate@outlook.com   Phone: 424-501-6046
Website: www.c2realestateinvestments.com

TJ Jordan

CHAPTER 8
DON'T ASK ME TO SETTLE

There was a little girl that wanted an Easter Egg hunt. I was sitting on a couch and noticed the Easter basket on the end table was full of eggs. I said, "Hey, here are the eggs right now." Why should she go through the trouble of finding them when they are right in front of her? Of course, the little girl wanted the fun of finding the Easter eggs. If we just gave any little kid the eggs without the hunt, they wouldn't want them. The eggs would have no meaning. They do not represent an accomplishment. Think of this: The child ends up with the same result at the end; A basket of eggs; whether through the struggle of the egg hunt, or by just receiving the egg from me without the struggle. The same basket of eggs. But there is a world of difference between these two identical baskets of eggs. Little kids will not stop until all the eggs are found and they will want to do it all over again right away. They don't want the hunt to be easy. They want difficulty. This illustration is deeper than you think. Two baskets of Easter eggs. They are the same eggs! However, one basket has no value and the other does. Let that sink in for a moment. Don't ask me to settle for the "free" eggs.

Now take the struggle of the egg hunt that offers excitement to kids and apply it to your life and your real adult problems. We want to avoid bad things and we should, but not every struggle should be avoided. Most pain or struggle comes at us no matter how cautiously we move through life. Little kids might be scratched by a bush when they eagerly plunge in their hand to grab a hidden egg. What egg has the most value? The one that caused a scratch on their arm. That egg looks no different than the others, but that one particular egg becomes the "trophy" egg and gets a prominent place on top of all the others. All those eggs look the same when they were on the end table. The value placed on some eggs is only because of the pain and struggle to find them. Just as kids proudly show all the eggs they hunted and found, the harder life is, the more value we place on the accomplishments we reach to achieve success. What gave our achievements value was the struggle to attain them. In the case of the Easter eggs both baskets look the same. However, for real adult accomplishments to be great, they only come with cost and struggle. In business the best achievements will come with the most efforts. Don't get easily discouraged when barriers show up on your journey to success. Expect barriers. They give you the value you so much want.

The barrier, pain, or struggle was not to keep us from our destiny. No, it was to help us get there.

Is it possible to accomplish something great without any pain or struggle? I don't think so. I cannot think of any accomplishment in my life or history that didn't include pain and struggle as a barrier. However, the barrier, pain, or struggle is not to keep us from our destiny. No, it was to help us get there. Some pains or struggles come at us out of left field with no warning. That pain can defeat us, or we can find the hidden talents already inside of us that the pain brought to the surface. Deep stuff, right?

Everyone has a gift or talent, something they are good at. I believe such gifts are God-given. If you don't believe your talent comes from God, that's okay It came from somewhere outside of you. Most often we don't use our gift to its full capacity. It lies dormant inside us. This gift peeks out every so often, but rarely do we fully realize what we can do unless something brings out this gift. That "something" is adversity. In my book, "You Can't Build a House on a Bridge," I greatly expand on what gives us value. What gives us a purpose in life? What makes our accomplishments valuable? I use the metaphor of a bridge as the process of life as we leave one part of our life that is crumbling and cross over to the next stage of our life where our destiny is waiting. We hold within us the ability to succeed by using our talent and gift, which are already resident on the crumbling side of our bridge. Only when you cross your bridge will you realize what you are worth. Don't ask me to settle for the crumbling side of my bridge.

Your current location is broken. You are not broken. You didn't arrive there broken and you're not leaving broken. Your current location may be full of negativity from people you thought had your best interests at heart. They think they do, but actually it is their interpretation of what is best for you.

Some people take a snapshot view of someone, a fleeting moment and apply that temporary view to an entire life. That fleeting moment may be the point you are going through your pain. The moment when you are in the process of crossing your bridge. Fleeting moments don't define us. All of us are a composite of our hopes, dreams, environment, self-doubt, self-imposed limitations, pain, and hidden talents. What wisdom we offer to others is filtered by everything that makes up our specific composite. Don't ask me to settle for a permanent definition of a temporary status of my life.

Wisdom is to not stick your hand in a snake pit. Fear is to always keep your hands in your pockets.

Some people live at some level of fear of what would happen if they fail at something. They fear stepping into their destiny, yet their gifted destiny is where they are supposed to be. When those people tell you what you should do, they are really expressing what they fear might happen, so they suggest you take the easy way and not step out, not take the chance you might fail. Some people live with a certain level of fear so long they think it is normal. They call it being cautious. Wary of the unknown. No, it's fear. Wisdom is to not stick your hand in a snake pit. Fear is to always keep your hands in your pockets.

In the movie "A League of Their Own", Tom Hanks portrays Jimmy Dugan, the manager of a women's baseball team named The Peaches. Some of the players complain about the grueling practice sessions. Tom Hanks's character responds, "If it were easy, everybody would do it. It's the hard that makes it great."[1] Life is hard and unfair. It is supposed to be. That's what keeps us moving and why there is a bridge available to get to your next stage in life. The pain gives you the strength and value to walk across. You can't just sit down and decompose. Don't ask me to settle for the easy way all the time. Sometimes I do like a break.

Some painful experiences are emotionally devastating-the "curl into a ball and hold your knees to your chest and groan" kind of pain. My divorce was that kind of pain. Paralyzing. I didn't eat. Lost fifteen pounds in less than ten days. The crippling pain lasted over a week. I felt I would never again be happy. A week of deep despair. I remember looking at some medicine bottles and wondering how many pills I would have to take to end my life. Fleeting thoughts like that came and went. My pain eventually evolved into a lower level pain that persisted for months. I lost my best friend and lover. I did not want to leave the life I had and cross over my bridge. Finally, I realized I had nothing left to stay for. I now know I can take a lot of crap and still get up. Looking back, I wonder if I could have figured out how to save my marriage. The answer is yes. I could have given up on my dream and settled for mediocrity and a failed career. I could have worked at something less than what I am gifted and created to do. Certainly, if my family were starving and if my two sons were young with no money coming in, any man would do whatever he had to do to put food on the table. That was not our issue at all. In a marriage we sometimes take turns holding each other up emotionally or financially.

Success for me came in cycles. I had a good long stretch of smooth existence separated by hard struggles. My last success and current one, took a long time. Throughout my career, I worked for large corporations and smaller video production houses. I made a good living for a long time. That industry changed quite a bit over the years. The high-paying jobs were fewer and fewer. I then started my own video production company and had some early success, but business dried up. I could have taken a job completely out of my area of expertise. A mediocre job that would have meant I gave up, wasted my gift, and settled for mediocrity. I wonder how long I would have lasted, knowing I had settled for something when I didn't need to. I did consider taking just any job. However, every time I got close to doing that, a mental brick wall would appear with a big sign that said, "No!" A few times I did apply for jobs I didn't want. I didn't get those jobs, but that didn't make me sad. I saw it as confirmation that I wasn't meant to settle for just any job. Don't ask me to settle for mediocrity.

Think of it like this: You have a disease and the doctor says there are two ways of dealing with your illness. One way is to settle for a partial healing, where you will not have full function of your body or be able to do everything you feel you can do, but at least the disease might be in remission. The second option comes with some unknowns, but there is a good possibility you might be able to fulfill all your dreams, you might regain full bodily functions, and you might be able to do what you're best at, what you were gifted to do. With those two alternatives, you might say, "I choose option two." Then the doctor says, "Wait a minute. Before you decide, option two has some unknowns and comes with risks, pain, and struggle." I choose option two anyway. I just cannot take option one. Don't ask me to settle for a mediocre decision.

It would be sad if after your pain and struggle, you settled for something you could have with no effort.

What some people correctly call mediocrity others call, "taking the safer decision". No, it's called mediocrity. The deep end of a pool is much more fun. Yes, there is more risk in the deep end. The shallow end is safer, but in reality, it's just standing and being wet. I could not settle for mediocrity. Then the excruciating pain came - the divorce, the emotional paralysis, the weight loss, the deep despair. Mediocrity is easy to attain. It would be sad if after your pain and struggle, you settled for something you could have with no effort. Mediocrity does not need a stretch. Does not need pain to get it. Just sit down and decompose. If you don't have a need to leave mediocrity, you will settle for it. This idea of "needing the need" is important. I believe we all have hidden talents ready to come out, but how do they come out? I feel I have a talent for writing. So why couldn't I have written my book before my marriage fell apart.

Throughout my book, "You Can't Build a House on a Bridge", I presented many illustrations asking whether accomplishments can happen without pain and struggle. Isn't there a better way to accomplish something without going through the pain? And I have said no. But I still wonder. Since I am a writer and I knew I was a writer before the pain of my divorce, why couldn't I have written my book before my divorce and maybe saved my marriage? Because there was no need in my life to write the book back then. Need came from the pain. The pain of my divorce gave me the need. The pain of the divorce gave me my value, my new identity, and the need to write everything down in my book called. I had to have all of those things in order to write the book. Yes, hidden talent comes out because of pain and struggle, perhaps only from pain and struggle.

If I had settled for mediocrity, my marriage might have lasted for a few more years. In reality my marriage was over; there was no going back. There was nothing to stay for. Nothing to settle for. It became a second-best marriage. My need was great, the pain was great, the value I achieved is great, my identity now is great, and I have used my gifts to write my book. Yes, you have ability and talent hidden inside of you but the only way for it to come out and show itself is to experience a need for it. The pain and struggle can give you that need. I may not like to say this or you may not like to hear it, but don't ask me to always settle for the least painful decision.

So, what happened when I refused to choose mediocrity? I became successful! Opportunities opened after a few months. My business took off. Timing is everything. This amazing business opportunity for my video production company was coming regardless of my state of mind. Let me say that again: This amazing business opportunity for my video production company was coming regardless of what state of mind I was in. I actually did little to bring about this new business opportunity. The only thing I did was not settle for mediocrity, knowing I would experience pain by choosing not to settle. I was willing to accept the pain with the hope or faith that I chose right. Choosing mediocrity would have eliminated this amazing opportunity from my future.

You have to appear in the place where your answer

will be. You must be available to see it. I was right where I needed to be when this opportunity came. How did I know where to be? I didn't. All that I did was to not give up. I did not settle. The increase came. Being mediocre will attract mediocre. It didn't matter if I stayed married or not, didn't matter if I was in deep despair or not. I was shown that I am not mediocre. If I had taken the easy, mediocre way out, I would not have met someone that started me down the road to my success. I would have been working at a job that I believe God did not want me to take. If I had settled for that job, I would not have met this person God prepared for me to meet. This key person didn't know what kind of role he would end up playing in my life. I didn't know. This person I met was in the midst of his own pain and issues. I felt compelled to check up on him from time to time, with no thought of what I might get out of it. I just thought it was right to show this person that someone cared besides family. If I had chosen mediocrity, I would still be in mediocrity now and would have missed the opportunity of my lifetime.

Here is some extra wisdom for you. This person that played such an important role in my life is a jerk. Don't assume opportunities only come wrapped in golden paper. Don't overlook, ignore, or fight against the jerks you encounter. Some jerks are smart. They may not make good friends, but they can be useful.

In business sometimes the battle to succeed seems so formidable you think about giving in and taking anything, a detour. Sometimes you may encounter this detour before you get to your final destiny. Detours are temporary. Detours may seem like giving in. They are not. Just a rest stop. This does not mean your dreams are gone. Detours are just the barriers we will face. Keep going. Don't ask me to settle for a temporary detour. I will find my way back even if the detour is longer journey.

You have to appear in the place you want to go before you get there.

As I looked back on this God-planned connection with this person, I wrote a deep, wise proverb: "You have to appear in the place you want to go before you get there." I made the turn toward my future. This turn, this key person, caused by a chance meeting, was in place before I got there. The right choice is not always the easy one. I believed in myself, and knew somehow, I needed to appear in the place I wanted to go before I got there. Of course, I didn't see my future, but I knew I had one. I had the faith to believe my future would be better even though I was not there yet. You don't always know where that place is, but you must believe there is a plan, a place, and someone you are supposed to be. I am not the owner of a failed video production company. I am not a powerless person curled into a ball on my bedroom floor. I chose to cross over the bridge to the next stage of my life. The pain was not meant to be avoided.

John Rohn said, "If you are not willing to risk the usual, you will have to settle for the ordinary."[2] Here is another quote I identify with by Vaibhav Shah: "Whenever you see a successful person, you only see the public glories, never the private sacrifices to reach them."[3] Why would someone choose pain over no pain? For me the pain of giving up on myself was something I could not do. Maybe I just chose what I thought was the pain I could handle. Or maybe what God thought I could handle. If I knew what I was going to face, would I have made the same decision? I don't know.

I don't like the cliché "If life hands you a lemon, make lemonade." A question I don't like: "What did you learn from your mistakes?" The first one trivializes your pain. The second one assumes the pain should have been avoided, and you try to squeeze out anything positive, so you say you "learned something." No, you will be changed into something better and stronger from pain. The purpose of pain is not to learn something but to become something new and better.

Don't fight against the realities of life and bad stuff that happens. Keep the memory of what you experienced before, know the hard part of life is just a bridge you must walk across and then look to that other side of the bridge and stretch toward your new destination.

A bridge takes you from one status of life to another. No one builds a house on a bridge. A bridge just connects things. You can't live on a bridge. When life is truly crumbling apart, like mine did, most people try to fix things where they are. Go ahead and try, but often we must head for the bridge to a new life. The bridge you must cross could be awful. You want what you are leaving behind, but it's gone. The bridge is where you don't want to be. You will find a new place to be. A new state of being you. You will be different.

How you react to the bridge determines how you will change. Don't fight against the realities of life and bad stuff that happens. Keep the memory of what you experienced before, know the hard part of life is just a bridge you must walk across and then look to that other side of the bridge and stretch toward your new destination. Make sure you have to stretch. Oliver Wendell Holmes Jr. said, "A mind that is stretched by a new experience can never go back to its old dimensions."

For me my defining moment was my divorce. For you it could be a job loss or an opportunity to make a huge change in your career. Many times a decision will show itself and you will know. This drawing below depicts a lotus flower. Not only is this flower beautiful but for some people it is a sacred symbol. Anyone can see how beautiful it is, but not everyone thinks of the mud it grows in. The mud is necessary for its life. Some people think of the lotus flower as a metaphor of life. "Out of the mud of life springs a flower." Nice thought, but I want to go deeper. Not only is mud required for the flower to grow but the mud had to appear first. Let's go deeper. When you start with the mud, the mud of life, you just have mud with no idea whether a lotus will bloom. You don't know the purpose of the mud at first. But you must have the mud and have it first without knowing why.

Be patient. Your bridge will appear. What worked on one side of your bridge may not work on the new side. Okay, let's just say it straight. It won't work. What you are leaving and where you are going are two different places, with two different sets of rules, two different sets of realities. When you get to where you are going, come flying at it with your arms spread wide as you embrace the new and improved you!

1. A League of Their Own, motion picture, directed by Penny Marshall, written by Babaloo Mandel and Lowell Ganz, starring Tom Hanks, Garry Marshall, Jon Lovitz, and Rosie O'Donnell, released July 1, 1992.

2. Jim Rohn, https://www.brainyquote.com/quotes/jim_rohn_/ '385514.

3. Vaibhav Shah, https://www.goodreads.com/quotes/ 1045015-whenever-you-see-a-successful-person-you-only- see-the.

TJ Jordan is winner of twelve national awards for video production over his many years as a television professional. Most of his awards were for producing and editing of video productions as well as his role as a writer for other business-related productions and television commercials. His book, "You Can't Build a House on a Bridge," is a unique look at the issues of life, the good and not so good and how all events of life make us what we are. The easy way is not always the best way. Terryjordan1@hotmail.com, bookstjjordan.com

Angela Day

CHAPTER 9
HOW FORGIVENESS CHANGED MY LIFE

Have you ever just prayed to God to have a real mother and daughter Relationship? Have you ever wondered why your mother didn't raise you but raised your other sisters and brothers? Have you ever wondered why she physically and mentally abused you but not your other siblings? Have you ever wondered why your biological mother would tell you things like: *You'll never amount to anything, you're dumb, stupid, and you'll never get pregnant, I wish I never had you, and you messed up my life."*

Yes, I heard these words a lot when my mother Betty and my sisters Fannie and Natalie came to live with my Aunt Rosa and me. I couldn't understand for the life of me what I did wrong. Why did my mother hate me so? It couldn't have been that I looked so much like her or that no matter how bad she treated me, I still tried to find ways to please her and make her happy. Why did my daddy James always come and play with me and teach me my ABC's, how to count to 100, my time tablets from 1 through 12, how to read and write before I even entered the first grade? But my mother never came to see me, or comb my hair, feed me, take care of me when I had the chickenpox, or when I got the measles. I don't ever remember her taking care of me when I was sick as a child.

Childhood

Now, let me take you back to a time where there were no Blacks or Black African Americans; only Colored, Negro or the N-word (Nigger) which was used quite frequently to describe my race. I lived in a small dominantly colored neighborhood where kids could freely play softball in the streets and called time out when the cars came driving down the road. It was a time where we only had two or three channels that we watched on a black and white television set that never stayed on all night because at midnight you could hear "The Star-Spangled Banner" and you knew it was getting ready to sign off and time for bed.

I remember the elderly grey-haired women sitting on their front porches during the day, dipping snuff, and others chewing tobacco and spitting in their tin can cup. They wore a long white slip up under their short-sleeved housecoats that buttoned or snapped up the front, with colorful flowers. They had two huge pockets, one on each side, where they kept their snuff, chewing tobacco, or Winston cigarettes. The older men would sit under the tree playing checkers and smoking cigars while drinking Budweiser beer and gazing at the young teenage colored girls walking through their yard in their hot pants thinking if they were only seventeen again.

Yes, those were the days when we could play games like hide and seek, dodge ball, and 1 2 3 red light in my mom's driveway and dance to Rufus Thomas singing on the radio "Do the Funky Chicken Now" or Earth Wind and Fire singing "Lets Groove tonight," or the O'Jays singing "Love Train." We would form the Soul Train line and my friends and I would take turns dancing down the middle of the driveway while trying to outdo each other.

I remember one day the watermelon man was in his truck going up the hill and his watermelons started falling off the back of it and rolling down. My mother and other adults begin to yell for us kids to catch those watermelons. We stopped playing hopscotch and took to the street with our arms stretch out wide, running to get in front of the watermelons to catch one before they busted open.

Yes, we did have fun, but we knew that we had to be home before the street lights came on or else. Sometimes, the neighbors would see us running and start yelling *run baby, run baby*, while laughing and making bets with each other to see if we made it back home on time. My mother Betty was known in the neighborhood for her cooking and having me and sometimes my sisters took plates over to those who were sick and shut-in. Mom always cooked more than enough food just in case some of her friends stopped by, or kids in the neighborhood were hungry. Everyone knew that they could come to Ms. Betty's house to get something to eat and if they needed to wash up, she would give them a bath towel, soap, toothbrush, and baking soda to brush their teeth with and Mum's deodorant. She was a hairdresser by profession and she'd have several of her church friend and neighbors come over and they would pay her to do their hair.

However, I didn't like for my mother to straighten my hair, especially when she was talking on the phone. She would pull my hair, push my head down and no matter how I held my ear, she would still burn me with the straightening comb and when I yelled, she'd hit me with a brush and tell me, "It's your fault for moving." I also, remember one day when she went to hit me with a hairbrush while doing my hair she said: "If I knew this brush wouldn't break, I would hit you with it." But, thank God the Afro hairstyle came out, and then the Jerri curl. Therefore, I no longer had to have my mother do my hair, burn my ears, and hit me. I was like Martin Luther King Jr when he said, *Free at last, free at last, thank God Almighty I'm free at last.* Yes, I was free, and it felt so good to do my own hair.

Yes, those were the days. Growing up in the south in a colored neighborhood we were taught to respect the elderly, our parents, and always give the greeting of the day no matter what. We didn't talk back, (well we'd mumble up under our breath, you know what I mean), or get caught out after the street light came on or use profanity. We wanted to be known for being excellent and well-behaved children in our community.

I remember if the neighbors caught us doing something wrong that they could give us a whipping and then tell our folks and we would get another one when we got home. I guess you're wondering, where was 911, child abuse hotline, or social services? Please, there was no such place, we just cried, sucked it up, wore pants and a long sleeve shirt the next day to keep everyone from looking at the welt marks on our legs and arms that came from the tree branch (called a switch) that they used to whip us with.

However, when I look back on it now, I can see where it helped me to be more outgoing. It allowed me to be able to talk to anyone without being scared. I can easily smile and give the greeting of the day, no matter what nationality. Because, we are all God's children and I want everyone to know that God loves us and He wants us to enjoy life, in abundance, to the full, until it overflows. Therefore, it doesn't make any sense for us to hate, despise, or be racist because of the color of our skin. God created us in His image and we all have a blood brought right to live a long healthy, happy, prosperous, and peaceful life.

But, if you're not willing to change the way you think, then you will never be able to change the way you live. You'll always be missing out on the beautiful things, places, and people that God wants you to have because you're not willing to renew your mind and accept that just because someone doesn't look like you or talk like you, it doesn't make you better than them. We must remember that God wants us to love our neighbors as we love ourselves and that doesn't mean the family or person who lives next door to you. It means every race, religion, and nationality. We are to treat them with kindness, humility, mercy, compassion, forgiveness, just like God gives to us every day.

Prejudice Has A Lesson

I can recall going on an interview at the First National Bank in Birmingham, Alabama with the rain pouring down so heavy and all the colored applicants dressed in lovely dresses, suits, and dress shoes all polished and shiny. However, the Caucasian applicants were in blue jeans, white tee shirts, and tennis shoes; yet they got the jobs. I remember hearing my interviewer say after taking all the tests for the job: "You came in the rain, you can type, you did well on the math test, and you can read and write." She then stated, "I can't believe how well you did."

I just sat there smiling and thinking, *of course I did. How could I apply for a job at a bank and not know how to do these things?* If you're wondering, did I get the job after two hours of testing? The answer is No. I didn't. She said, "Her colleague had hired someone else and she was sorry."

But you know, I grew up being talked down to and made to feel that I would never amount to anything because of my skin color and being a woman. My mother even told me that I was dumb, stupid, and would never amount to anything. She also said the same thing about my son. But you know, the more I was told that the more I studied and proved her wrong. I received good grades in Junior High and High School. I was always on the Honor Roll. I asked for a tutor to help me with Algebra I, II, and Trigonometry when I had problems with the formulas. I would stay up late studying sometimes to 4:00 am, while my classmates were already in bed asleep.

I was determined to learn and I received all A's. I say this because it's easy to get discouraged when your mother and people who look down on your race tell you that you'll never make it. But you've got to gather your courage and prove to them that they're wrong and you will succeed. Because you are beautiful, intelligent, creative, and you can learn. It might take you a little longer, but don't give up or lose hope. Stay in the race and be like the tortoise who kept his pace and at the end, he won over the rabbit because the rabbit was too overconfident. His arrogance and pride caused him to lose the race to the tortoise. Therefore remember, the Bible says, "The race isn't given to the swift but he that endureth to the end."

Now, don't get me wrong, being prejudiced against was not an easy process for me to change. I couldn't stand for anyone, especially Caucasians, to speak to me like I didn't matter and treat me like a second-class citizen. I couldn't understand for the life of me why they didn't like my color? Mainly when they would lay in the sun to get my shade. It just didn't make any sense to me. But the more I worked with them I found out that from generation to generation they were raised to hate colored people; in fact, to hate anyone who was not like them or had their social status.

Also, they concluded that colored people weren't smart because our brains aren't fully developed and that's why we are only suitable for hard labor. But this was nothing but lies and excuses to hold us back from getting decent-paying jobs, positions in government, being pilots and officers in the military, and receiving a higher form of education at well-known colleges and universities.

Next, I discovered that some had serious issues such as insecurities, loneliness, not skinny enough, jealousy, not pretty enough, not smart enough for their families. Also, less athletic abilities, addictions to a different type of drugs, and family secrets that caused them to have unhealthy lives and relationships. I realized that they needed to be loved and accepted for who they are just like I did. But to receive love, you must learn how to love and respect yourself and know what God says about you and what it means to love and forgive the Godly way.

New Beginning, That First Step

As I began to study the Bible and hear the word of God in a word church, I learned that God says "We are His children, sons, and daughters, kings and queens, ambassadors for Christ, heirs of Abraham." I learned that through Jesus' death, we were adopted into the royal family and were no longer Gentiles. Plus, we could now have a relationship with God because of Jesus Christ's great sacrifice. I learned that God loves me, and He will never leave me nor forsake me. He is my Shepherd, My Warrior God, My Healer, My Jehovah-Jireh (My provider).

First, I had to make up my mind to forgive my family. After that, I prayed, believed, and spoke the word only in my life to forgive my mother, son, and sisters who had caused me so much pain in my life. I had to stop seeing and thinking of myself as a victim and see myself as a child of God. Because just like God forgave me with a sincere heart, I had to do the same for my family.

Second, I had to come out of my comfort zone and do things I wouldn't normally do, such as initiating the first move towards repairing my relationship with my family.

Next, I had a private one on one talk with each of them. I told them to tell me everything that they wanted to say to me and I would do the same and we would never bring up the past again. I wanted to know their thoughts about me and what was keeping us from being a family. After we talked they all said, "You love the church more than me." But I told them, That's not right. You should be glad that I'm in church and love God because if I didn't, I would have never returned. However, because I desire to live for God, I'm here willing to work on having a family relationship."

I knew that I had to start spending more quality time with them to show that they did matter. I started planning different events such as bowling, going to the theatre, and Friday movie night in which I brought pizza, wings, sodas, and movies over. I played bingo, spades, and gin rummy with my family. I would invite them to see Tyler Perry plays and purchase tickets when he came to our hometown to perform. I invited them to church and I also offered to pick them up and take them. I took them out to dinner or brought dinner over on Sunday's, so my sister Fannie wouldn't have to cook.

I let them know when my church had carnivals, family movie night, comedy night, plays, and Christian concerts. I would give them free church calendars and ink pens that I had received for the New Year. I kept them informed of all the events that I felt they would like to attend. I would either purchase food and drinks for them or give them the money for it.

Everything I did for my family was to let them know that I was sincere in having a wholesome family relationship. But in the end, I did it to honor God. I knew that if I wanted my family to see that their perceptions of me was wrong, I had to continue to come out of my comfort zone and show that my love and concern for them was real.

I stopped speaking negatively and gossiping about my family. I started praying for them and speaking long life, prosperity, wisdom, and that they were bible carrying believers of God, trusting and doing His word. Because, if you want your family and friends to be saved, delivered, and serve God, then you must be that light that shines through the darkness to let them see God in you.

God tells us to forgive those who trespass against us. His word in Luke 6:37 (KJV) "Judge not, and ye shall not be judged: condemn not, and ye shall not be condemned:

forgive and ye shall be forgiven. "Therefore, as children of God, sons, and daughters, we have to realize that it's not about us, it's about honoring God. We don't judge, we don't discriminate. We forgive, we show God's love, and we do it to honor God because when we honor God, He will honor us.

I didn't get this overnight. I cried, had pity parties, was very prideful, and had sleepless nights, as I tried to hold on to my pain. But as I begin to let the word of God minister to my heart, mind, and soul, I could no longer have it reside in me.

Next, after I asked God for forgiveness towards Him and my family, I noticed that they begin to enjoy being at church with me. They would always ask me to let them know when we were having any events so they could come out. We smiled, laughed and enjoyed each other's company and I even introduce them to my Pastor and friends at church.

My relationship with my family began to turn around for the better. I learned to set boundaries and not let them use my being a Christian to help them pay their bills or anything else anymore. Since I didn't feel guilty, ashamed or obligated anymore, I felt my life had no meaning.

I went to financial counseling along with regular counseling for myself and I learned that I wasn't responsible for my family's debt. I read books, listened to CD's, and watched videos about managing your finances, coming out of debt, and setting boundaries. I learned how to say no to my family. I stopped letting them use the Christian card, the manipulation card, the blood card, and the sister card. I learned that if I wanted to get out of debt, I had to change my way of thinking to change my way of living.

Therefore, as I began to apply what I learned and what God began to show me about giving where I was, to come out of debt, the *Debt Reduction Diva* was born. After successfully getting my finances back on track, I decided to help others do the same.

Forgiveness was my key to allowing myself to prosper in the area of relationships. Education about finances was the way I was able to open up to financial prosperity.

If there are people in your life you feel angry with, carry a grudge against, or feel resentful towards, forgiveness may be the answer. If you are tired of living from paycheck to pay check, working two or three jobs to make it and still in debt, tired of your family and friends using those cards I listed above to get money from you, or just need to learn how to set boundaries to have a more successful financial life, I encourage you to educate yourself about finances.

And remember, if I was able to do it, you can too.

Angela Day is known as the *Debt Reduction Diva*. She helps people come out of Debt by helping them understand that money is a tool and if you don't know how to use it then it will use you. Her mission statement is: When you change your way of Thinking then you can change your way of Living. Angela offer debt reduction strategies and you can contact her at: Email- author@angelalday.com,
Facebook- How to Love the Hell Out of Folks
Facebook- How to Be Debt Free

Michael Jay Hollander

CHAPTER 10
I AM THE WALRUS

It was a warm clear Saturday night in Douglaston, Queens, NY and the sky was filled with bright, shiny stars. Zip's parents were out of town so it was time for a summer house party before college started up again. It was meant for maybe twenty people of our inner circle, but word quickly spread throughout the bars and other neighborhoods about the party.

Zip had lost control of his party and his house. As the night went on, there were over seventy people there and we hardly recognized most faces in the crowd. It was bedlam with wall-to-wall people smoking and drinking in every room. The music was turned up high, as Led Zeppelin screamed from the living room speakers. Everywhere you turned it was smoky and stuffy and filled with the unrecognizable. I ventured outside squeezing past more unknown faces blocking the front door. I needed the fresh air to cool down. As I exited, I realized I didn't recognize anyone hanging out on the stoop.

The summer evening breeze on my face felt invigorating. I was standing at the bottom of the steps just outside the front door, still enjoying the break from all the chaos and heat inside. I started to head back in for some more vodka-soaked watermelon. As I made my way to the top step of the stoop, I hear, "What the fuck you looking at?"

I honestly only remember looking up towards the front door, quizzically gazing at all the unknown faces, but apparently, I had made eye contact with this dude's girlfriend. Being the smart ass that I was, I responded, "Not much dude." Next thing you know I get cold-cocked; a right hook solidly connected, rattling my jaw. My knees wobbled, but I didn't fall down. With my legs weak, Sal the punk, scooped me up. I felt like I was getting ready for a World Wrestling Association body slam. Time froze. Everything and everyone started moving in slow motion. Sal had me in a grip with one arm clenched over my shoulder and another between my legs.

He lifted all 140 lbs. of me high into the air. Zip was standing right on the other side of the screen door watching. When Zip and I made eye contact my eyes pleaded for some assistance. In what felt like a hapless eternity, the punk took two steps forward lifted me and tossed me over the black rod iron railing off the porch and down to the bottom of the driveway. I landed flat on my back on top of two aluminum garbage cans and somehow like a cat I managed to bounce to my feet. As I shook the cobwebs from my cloudy mind, I was still in shock from what had just happened. I was just punched in the face for the first time in my life. The good news is I survived, and it was over.

I had never been in a real grown-up fist fight. I was still groggy from the punch to the face and the eight-foot drop. My Spidey senses didn't tell me that there was more to come. As I stood alone, trying to assess what the fuck just happened and trying to comprehend the situation, I saw two guys charging straight for me. Shit, I thought I am in trouble. When they got up on me, I started aimlessly throwing punches to defend myself. Oh man, where were the troops? I needed my boys. I was bum-rushed and my back was shoved up against the garage. Still flailing away in self-defense mode, biding time trying to survive my attackers, I ended up back on the ground. Let me tell you this is no place to be. I curled up to protect myself, but a foot connected to my chin. *Are they stomping on me? Kicking me in the face while I am down? When is this going to end?*

Finally, the beating abruptly ended. I slowly rose up and calmly walked the twenty feet of shame to the top of the driveway leaving little splatters of blood behind. I tasted the blood in my mouth, and felt the blood from my chin dripping to the sidewalk. I suffered a cut inside on my lower lip and my jaw was starting to swell. I was thinking, *Well, I survived, life will go on as it always does. I just withstood a beat down by two punks. I am standing, walking and talking, and not in too much pain. The best news was no ambulance is necessary. I just need some ice.* I stood at the top of the driveway still shaking off the bats in the belfry when I realized my other childhood friend Gary, who had pulled them both off of me, was asking me if I was okay. All of a sudden, I hear a girl say, "You bloodied my boyfriend." She proceeds to squarely kick me in my nuts. *What the fuck!*

Now I am getting kicked in the balls by some crazy chick after I sustained a beating from two dudes. Round three, enough was enough. My brain ordered my legs to flee the scene and protect my future children. Though I didn't realize it at the time, this was the beginning of the end of my friendship with all those guys. This trauma only fed into my insecurities and self-doubt. I feared my friends viewed me as a pussy for running away because I'd had enough. I couldn't face them after that night.

That moment is still a vivid memory and haunts me to this day. That night changed my life in so many ways. One of the sad results was I lost my best friend Cole in that fight. Two weeks after that fateful evening, I went off to the State University of New York at New Paltz. We all went from hanging out almost every day to not seeing each other before I set out to college. I left the neighborhood for good. My circle was broken by my own insecurities. We were a close group of kids for so many years and I let that slip away.

After that night, I learned how to fight and defend myself. While I was still a fragile little man on the inside, I became more of an extraverted tough guy on the outside. I would project toughness so it would cover up my weakness and insecurities. I studied martial arts and took some boxing classes on and off over the next few years.

My high school days in New York were not memorable. It was a tough period for me. Not only did I have ADHD and failed to make high grades but I also suffered from an inferiority complex that still besets me today. It's easy for me to get thrown into a personal purgatory of self-doubt in many situations. I often think how much better I would feel if I were capable of brushing these situations aside and go on about my day without doubting myself and my life.

I was slow to mature and slow to develop. My insecurity caused me feelings of anger, resentment, and jealousy. It held me back from succeeding in relationships and career choices. Much of my personality is based on my insecurities. Still, they created who I am today. A person experiencing high levels of insecurity may often experience a lack of confidence facing many aspects of life. It may be difficult for that person to form lasting relationships or attend to daily tasks, due to a self-perception of helplessness or inadequacy. This certainly describes me but I keep working on myself.

I've deeply pondered the nurture aspect of the nature vs. nurture question. Who would I be today if my Papou had lived and been an influence in my early developing years? How different would my life, personality, past, present and future be if circumstances had been drastically different forty-seven years ago? Who would I be today if my father had taken a job in a small town called Waltham, Massachusetts just eleven miles east from Boston? Would I have been a doctor or lawyer or a gang member selling coke and ending up in prison? Would Sam Adams Boston Lager be my beer of choice? What would a Boston accent sound like coming from my mouth? The questions can go on and on for infinity. Did you have any of those kinds of moments or decisions that would have changed everything? After years of feeling insignificant with an abundance of insecurities, I just ponder what would life be like now if....

Life was about to change for me. I made new friends and met two girls. During my first semester of Queensborough Community College in 1980, Sandra just walked straight up to me in the halls and planted the most amazing kiss I had ever experienced. I think I instantly fell in love and I didn't even know her name. I had never even heard her voice. I opened my eyes from that kiss, dazed and confused. As our lips parted, she took a step back, I looked into her beautiful face and noticed her long black hair, big brown eyes, and luscious full lips smiling at me. I was hers. And she knew it. That semester belonged to us. It was with her I had my first intimate experience. After my time dating Sandra expired, I moved on and had a fantastic girlfriend named Mary.

After dating Mary on and off for seven years, we got engaged; but like our past seven years of on again/off again, we couldn't stay committed and called the wedding off six months before the event. Here I wonder what life would have been like for the both of us if we went through with the marriage. Who would we be today - where would we be living - what about having children together? I lost touch with her and I hope she is incredibly happy somewhere.

Sometime during the following semester, I met another

girl in one of my classes named Sharon and we got to talking. It turns out she was in the student government holding a position in the Senate. She asked me if I would be interested in maintaining a seat in the Senate as someone had just dropped out. I told her I was intrigued. I was never really a part of any group, other than sports teams. She suggested that I meet her in the student government building the following Wednesday. She cued me on what to say to members of the Senate. After a short interview, they asked me to leave the room so they could democratically take a vote. Of course, my insecurities were kicking in on all gears. I was wondering, "What if I don't get in?" "Why didn't they like me?" ...what if what if what if..." They quickly called me back into a large room with a long conference table where the twelve members of the Senate sat. They congratulated me as the newest member of the student government. They handed me a parking pass to the best parking lot on campus. Let the perks begin.

As the semester was coming to a close, I connected with a lot of people in the student government. Senator Robert Bass asked me to run on his ticket as his Vice President. I was honored and excited. It was a big deal to hold these two prestigious positions. We formed a party and I came up with our tagline, Students United Now, the SUN party. We ran against a close friend of mine named Tony Schlachter. When Tony's party was defeated, he ended up back in the Senate where we would closely work together and become lifelong friends.

Issues of importance would take place in our meetings. We had financial budgets to allocate. We had funds to equitably distribute amongst all fifty clubs that asked for money to hold special events. We attended meetings with the faculty and the College President. Most importantly, we were the voice of all QCC students, and we represented them proudly. The prominent issue students brought to our attention was the dark and dangerous parking lots.

During a faculty meeting, we explained that students attending night-time classes needed a well-lit parking lot in order to return safely to their vehicles. They agreed and had lights installed for evening classes and social events that were held on campus.

As VP, I oversaw all clubs and activities. When a certain club needed financing for an event, they would make an appointment and meet with the me and the allocation committee. We would vote how to distribute funds fairly to each club. In return for representing each and every club and aiding their financial success, clubs invited me to their meetings when something special was happening. The food club was one of my favorites. The Russian club threw the best parties.

We had so many perks, life was good. We once booked Meatloaf to perform for the entire community and Jorma Kaukonen to perform on another occasion. I felt important which made me feel big on the inside. I was like Norm on *Cheers*, everybody on campus knew my name. One of the best fringe benefits was student government's power to allocate funds to itself and hold a weekend-long team-building conference. My first year we took the entire student government to the Rocking Horse Dude ranch in Upstate Highland, NY. I had a glimpse into my future which was riding and loving horses.

With the monies we allocated, the ski club took its club members and invited everybody from the student government to join them for a day trip to Killington Ski Resort in Vermont. The resort known for its mountains and great skiing, has six peaks at 4,241 feet of elevation with over 3,000 feet of vertical drops. It was a cold and blistering morning with extremely high winds. We had to suffer through an ice storm, but we were all determined to get a day of skiing in. I was on the lift chair, high above the white tree tops, enjoying the view below as the skiers zoomed down the snow-covered mountain.

All of a sudden, the chair lift came to a screeching halt.

With the wind zipping and the ice falling, we quickly froze. I lost feeling in both hands and my toes went numb inside my ski boots. We sat rocking on that lift chair for twenty minutes wondering what the hell was going on. Finally, we started moving and got to the top of the mountain. We couldn't ski fast enough to get to the bottom and into the ski resort where a warm fire and hot chocolate were screaming our names.

As we made our way down the mountain, we noticed ski patrol had gathered, working on some injured people. One body was already strapped in the gurney and heading down the slopes for medical treatment. It turns out that a single empty chairlift had amassed heavy ice on its cables. In the high winds, that chair slid down along the cable into the chair below which carried two people from our group. They extended their skis outward to prevent the chair from crashing into them; this created a chain reaction. The empty chair fell from its grip, dropping twenty feet and crashing onto the slope below. The chair carrying our students slid into another chair of two horrified skiers, ejecting the occupants of both chairs onto the snow below. Our skiers suffered from broken ankles and severe compound fractures. It was a long, quiet ride back home with two empty seats in the back of the van.

In 1983, during my senior year, we attended an award ceremony at Tavern on the Green in Central Park where I received a prestigious award. The Faculty Board voted me winner of the John F. Kennedy Memorial Award for demonstrating outstanding college and community leadership, as well as scholastic achievement. Early in my senior year I was sent to Washington, D.C. to run for New York State Representative of the CUNY (City Universities of New York). I had to get on stage and give an impromptu speech on why I should be chosen. I did not win that election, but it provided a bit more growth into better self- understanding, confidence and self-acceptance. I wonder whether I would have entered a life of politics if

I had won that election.

I have never stopped learning. I went back to college twice, in my 30's and again in my 40's. I studied early childhood education and child psychology to be a better parent and to have a successful business. When I was a salesman, I studied how to sell. When I owned a horse, I studied horsemanship. When I decided to write a book, I researched writing. It is important to continually grow, sometimes alone and best times with a willing partner.

I have come to realize that there is no such thing as bad luck or good luck for that matter. It was just my insecurities, not believing in myself and a fear of failure that held me back. That being said, I am a believer in fate and destiny. Life is decided by the choices and paths you make and take. It comes down to the individual deciding on what rules they want to play by in the game of life. Every person creates their own future, past, and present with the choices, paths, and daily decisions they make. Some events work out, some do not. It is what you learn from the failed choices and how one uses that knowledge and experience to grow, change and make your own life better. I have always stressed to my girls to make good decisions and not do anything stupid. So far so good. If you don't want to be ordinary, exude confidence, accomplish goals, and put yourself out there.

Looking back on my life, I realized that I have experienced the extraordinary and that being ordinary most times may not be such a bad thing.

After weeks of daily morning meditation releasing the negative energy and freeing my mind, I woke up one morning no longer felt sorry for myself and my depression was gone. Meditation made my mind calmer and more focused. Ten-minute breathing meditation helped me overcome stress and I found some inner peace and balance. When I meditate, I remove all the poison from my body.

When I had an epiphany of self-discovery, I came to

terms with who I am, and how the trials and tribulations influenced my development that molded me into the person I am today. It made me question and research the nature versus nurture debate. Whether human behavior is determined by the environment, either prenatal, genetically or during a person's life. Nature is what we think of as pre-wiring and is influenced by genetic inheritance and other biological factors. Nurture is generally taken as the influence of external factors after conception e.g. the product of exposure, experience and learning on an individual.

How you are raised, where you were raised and by whom really make who you are. I have noticed a vast difference in people who grew up on the West Coast compared to those on the East Coast. Growing up in New York you need to have moxie and street smarts, eyes behind your head, be sharp on your toes. You must avoid being taken advantage of on a daily basis which can sometimes lead to distrusting others.

For the most part, I have stayed true to myself. I do find myself sometimes holding back and biting my tongue, trying not to be over the top offensive. I am a rude, crude dude with an attitude. I like to speak my mind and tell off-putting jokes. Sometimes people just don't get who I am. I just rub some people the wrong way, and I have to live with that. To really know me is to love me. I am extremely sensitive, capable of love and affection, sentimental and a hopeless romantic.

I saw how I had always seen the glass as half empty, not appreciating the things I had. I took for granted all the blessings in my life and all that I have accomplished and achieved. If I didn't even know myself, how could I expect anybody else to truly know me? I now look for spiritual guidance and inner strength in making me a better, stronger, relaxed, patient and gracious person.

The Bridge
by Michael Jay Hollander

Two paths to take, which shall I follow?
The road to a small village or the road which leads to the
bridge? We already know with experience what we get within
the village. It's the other side of the bridge that is so
mystifying and seems so far away

The easy road or the long road whichever road
we must walk alone following the path of the unknown

It's all about strength and courage. Be brave. Take baby steps
towards the bridge

On the other side, destiny awaits
What will I find?
Will it be as beautiful as what was behind me? Time to cross
the bridge Time will tell

Michael Jay Hollander was born in 1962 in Brooklyn, New York. He is
a sports enthusiast and an avid traveler. He loves a good book and a
short nap in his hammock. Michael is Passionate about Scuba Diving
and horse camping with his beautiful wife Sonya and their two
Mustangs. He also enjoys long walks on the beach and trail hikes
with his dog, Brooklyn. He has two grown daughters Chase and
Jenna living in the San Francisco Bay area. Michael is also author of
"A Memoir of an Ordinary Guy, It's All Good Man" which can be
purchased at Amazon.

Mari Mitchell

CHAPTER 11
AUTHENTICITY - MY PATH TO PROSPERITY

Allowing yourself to prosper or letting yourself prosper, takes courage, practice, and loving yourself enough to trust your own instincts.

Allowing myself to prosper, in all areas of my life is a continuing journey. When I first heard the concept of allowing what I want into my life, I thought it couldn't be that easy. I had always believed you had to work hard for everything; relationships, finances, health, and even spiritual development. That's what I had done my entire life. Work hard.

As a child I had a very demanding and strict father. I now understand that his intention was getting my sister and I to be successful, free of financial worries, and happy. But back then I didn't like it. I became very much a people pleaser and pleasing him was a necessity. I got straight A's all through high school, giving every project, assignment, or task I did my best effort. I did have academic achievements to show for all my hard work, but I looked forward to graduating so life could be easier. Life didn't become easier for me. It became hard and even harder as I pushed myself to do everything that not only everyone else expected of me, but things that I expected of myself. Everything, had to be perfect. Everything.

Eighteen years later, now married with three children, that type of thinking and lifestyle lead me to feeling overworked, underappreciated, resentful, and exhausted. I was not Superwoman even though I tried to show the world around me that I was. Keeping up the household, taking care of most of my kid's needs, teaching Sunday School, volunteering for the school PTA, along with parents that needed to be driven everywhere because they did not drive, were my responsibility. Not to mention baking for school functions, helping my kids with projects, volunteering at school and church, the list was endless. I felt like I was on a merry-go-round and couldn't get off. I was heading towards burnout, but didn't know how to stop. It took me seventeen years of married life to come to the place where I was so unhappy, so empty and void of inspiration, so numb, that I had to make a change. The need to create a life where I felt better overcame the need to be perfect and have a perfect life.

I didn't know whether there could be a better, less stressful life for me. But I was willing to separate from my husband and move two hundred miles away to find out. I was too busy putting our house on the market, packing, and preparing the kids for the separation to feel any fear of the future. I did what had to be done and found myself, just a week before Christmas, in a new apartment of my own with my two daughters. I'll never forget when I unlocked the door and the girls went in to check the place out. They both started crying and saying, "We want to go home, Mommy." It broke my heart, but I knew this was the right path for me. Having pulled myself away from all the stressors in my life except my two daughters, felt like boulders were lifted from my shoulders. I could breathe again. I could do pretty much what I wanted. I would add "I could be me," but I hadn't found my authentic self quite yet. It felt good to be more relaxed about everything. I had always been so uptight, rigid and demanding. (Remind you of anyone I mentioned in my third paragraph?). I found that I no longer knew how to really enjoy life and all the little pleasures life affords. I very gradually began to loosen up and get in touch with the child inside of me. I hadn't let her come out to play in a very long time. At this point in my life It took focus to be more childlike, open and playful. But doing so brought many happy experiences to me.

I was now in a relationship with a man who was so carefree and spontaneous that he brought out that little girl in me who was so ready to come out and play. I was learning to just have fun, be more open, spontaneous. I found that I had so many rules for myself, my life, and my daughters. Unnecessary, ridiculous rules that did not serve me or them. I threw them out and stepped into more freedom than I had ever known. I was able to enjoy my daughters more; to be less demanding of them, more accepting and encouraging. I was able to be a tad more accepting of myself and others. I had a very long way to go, but it was a good start for me. I eventually learned to just frolic, enjoy the day, and let my kids enjoy themselves instead of trying to control their every move. It took me much longer than I would have hoped, but I began opening myself up to prosper in the area of family and relationships. I say opening up because there was SO much more for me to learn, so much more opening up and allowing, and so much more joy that I would experience in my life.

A year into the relationship I was feeling the wrath of my boyfriend's rage. He was verbally abusive and overly critical. Nothing I did could please him and I blamed myself for his angry outbursts trying to be perfect so he would be happy. It was like that children's rhyme. *When she was good, she was very, very good but when she was bad, she was horrid.* That was him. And the horrid behavior showed itself more and more often.

Fast forward six years into that relationship; I was feeling unloved, unappreciated, taken advantage of and had very little self-esteem left. I knew I was unhappy, (crying myself to sleep almost every night attested to that), but all I could think about was that first year we were together and how perfect everything was. I believed that if I tried hard enough and did everything perfectly, I could get us back to that. It took six years for me to finally realize the relationship was not the right one for me. This relationship, the first relationship after separating from my husband was one of my biggest mistakes ever AND one of my best choices. The worst because I suffered so much in those six years all the while trying to fix it. The best, because after six years of misery I was determined to find a new way of living, a joyful way of living. I knew it was possible. I just didn't know how.

Before breaking up with him for good I had to prepare myself. I had no friends, no interests, no hobbies besides what we did together. (Which of course were his hobbies, friend and interests). Instinctively I knew that my first step was making friends and doing things I loved to do. I decided to find a social group to join and in a Google search I found MeetUp.com. A site where you could find activities that you enjoy and do them with other people who have the same interests. I joined a couple of groups, a writer's group in a town nearby and a social group that met five minutes from my house. This was my first step in allowing myself to prosper in the area of friendship and relationships. It wasn't easy. Especially since the first time I tried to attend a writer's meeting I couldn't find the coffee shop they met at. And the first two times I tried attending the social group meeting I couldn't find them either. But I persisted and the third time I tried, I was finally able to get a hold of the organizer on the phone and he told me exactly where they were sitting in the restaurant. I had to be bold and introduce myself to everybody. I had to come out of the cave of loneliness I had put myself into and begin interacting socially again. It felt great!

The writer's group gave me a beautiful outlet for my creativity to flow. I discovered that I loved writing and it made me feel great. (I still feel that way about writing.) At the social group I clicked immediately with a woman and we became friends. Now I had someone to go out with and do things with. Slowly I became more outgoing and confident. I was having fun and I was happier, even though I was still in that bad relationship. My boyfriend noticed the changes in me and as I created my own space for being me, he started making some changes for the better. For a second, I thought maybe the relationship was salvageable. But then I reminded myself that I knew he would never truly change. I was done.

My confidence and more happy moments allowed me to distance myself from him. I was still seeing him, but my every thought and breath was no longer about him. This felt good. But I didn't feel ready to break up with him yet. I remembered the agony I had felt the first time I broke up with him (for only four months) and I wasn't ready to face that kind of pain again.

It took several months and one more fight with him for me to say it was over. I knew he probably didn't believe that I had broken up with him for good, but the next morning when he came over to my place to get some of his things, I handed him my key to his apartment and told him to leave my keys on the kitchen counter. I still remember the look of surprise on his face as he realized I was not changing my mind this time. I felt empowered, exhilarated, free. I immediately made plans with new Meetup friend for that evening. That feeling carried me through the day and night. The next morning, I was feeling the brunt of the breakup. It sunk in that I wouldn't be spending any more time with a person I still loved dearly. I was briefly tempted to call him and say I had changed my mind. But, as I thought about how having him in my life really affected me, I stuck to my decision to stay completely away from him. I'm not going to tell you that it was all butterflies and sunshine. I missed him so deeply that my hearts literally hurt in my chest. I made myself drive the long way home so I wouldn't have to go by his place. I tried to put him out of my mind, but he was still in there, planted like a bad weed with thick roots. It took determination and focus to stick to my decision and as I did so day after day, month after month I made progress.

One day, after getting home from an event with my social group, I realized that I hadn't thought about my ex-boyfriend ALL day. Not once. That was huge for me and I smiled at myself. I knew at that moment that there was no turning back. And the future looked brighter than I could have imagined.

No, Prince Charming did not ride up on his white horse and sweep me off my feet. I regularly had one -time dates with men from a dating site I had joined and even dated a couple of the guys briefly. But I had no committed relationship for a couple of years. During this time was my chance to keep working on myself and learn how to allow love into my life. I still made many mistakes when it came to dating. I put too much focus on HIM and too little on ME. I waited around not making plans in case some guy wanted to take me out. I spent way too much time looking for love instead of enjoying my life. After two years of internet dating and not finding the "one" I was discouraged and frustrated. I still believed that true love was there for me, but trying as hard as I could to find him was not working.

This is where the allowing comes in. I've learned through years of practicing the "Law of Attraction" that we attract what we are transmitting to the Universe. If I'm transmitting fear of abandonment, I'm going to attract men who will abandon me. If I'm transmitting love, love will be attracted to my life. The realization of this concept came way before I was able to apply it to my life. I knew what I had to do. Focus on love; loving myself, loving my children, my grandchildren, my mom, my friends and be as happy as I could each day. Doing this was a challenge. It was easy for me to get depressed when it seemed like everyone around me had a partner and I was alone.

It took me several more years of practicing healthy relationship behaviors and practicing how to allow love to come into my life before I could see and feel some real changes. Fully accepting myself with all my flaws was my first step. That wasn't something that happened in a month or two. I did many exercises, journaled constantly, and became aware of my self-talk. It amazed me the terrible things I said about myself to myself in my inner dialogue. I practiced setting boundaries with people, learning to say no instead of saying yes to please others, taking time for self-care instead of taking care of everybody's needs before taking care of myself.

In fact, I was doing so well that a met a man and married again. The marriage only lasted just over four years. I wasn't really paying attention to who he really was when we met and started dating. Once we were married (a little over a year after we started dating), he wanted to make me be who HE wanted me to be. Although I was authentic enough by then to stay me, this causes much friction in the marriage. It felt like a constant tug of war and I was so weary of fighting to be ME.

Once the divorce was final, I moved to California. It was June, 2015. For more than a year I focused on me. No dating, no internet dating sites, no striving to find a man. I knew that I would eventually want a man to share my life with, but that wasn't my main focus. I focused on my coaching, my radio show, my writing, on enjoying the beach that was just minutes from my home. I enjoyed the outdoors like I never could in Florida because of the incessant heat. I joined some meetup groups again to get out and have some fun. I made a couple friends and met them for coffee, wine or dinner. We went out together and enjoy so many lovely things. I loved my life and my heart began healing.

Just before Valentine's Day 2016 I felt it. I knew I was ready to let romantic love into my life again. I let this desire go up into the Universe as my request. I now truly believed that what I had asked for would come to me. All I had to do was allow.

I decided to sign up for a couple of internet dating sites. It all seemed very exciting and I was flattered by the men contacting me. But, within a couple of months I was discouraged and frustrated. I discovered that most of the men on these sites were scammers. (They were just there to try to get money from whoever they set their sights on.) The others were flaky. One day they were texting me non-stop, the next they wouldn't respond to my text messages - one day they were talking about meeting me, then when I responded with my availability they never messaged back.

Having been practicing for so many years how to feel as happy as I could in order to keep my vibration up, I knew that these negative feelings I had about the internet dating sites were keeping me down. I decided I would close my two accounts. I told God/Universe that although I believed it could be possible for Him to connect me with my perfect match through these sites, it was just too disheartening for me, so He would have to come up with another way to made the connection. The next day I was on one of the sites getting ready to delete my account when a message came in. It was very short and simple: "Hi, how are you doing today?" I looked at his profile. He had only one profile picture and it wasn't at all flattering. He did have a great smile though. I thought he might be a scammer since he had only one photo and a mostly blank profile, but I was inspired to respond to him. I sent him a short and simple message. Then he asked if we could text instead of using the site messaging service and I agreed. We were texting for a bit and I wanted to qualify this man as to whether he was a scammer of not. So, I asked him to take a picture of himself right now and text it to me. He said the camera on his phone was broken. There was my proof. I was certain he was a scammer and I told him so by text. He asked me why I thought that and I told him. Then I said, "If you're not a scammer, call me right now." And he did. Once we were talking on the phone, I realized he was just a guy looking for love and not a scammer at all. I profusely apologized to him and we hit it off so nicely on the phone that he asked to meet the following Saturday.

That was two and a half years ago and my guy is the sweetest, most loving, agreeable, considerate man I have ever been in a relationship with. Yes, he does have faults. So do I. There is no perfect, but there is the opportunity to experience love, joy, laughter, fun, passion. There is the opportunity to enjoy each other's company and co-create a life that we both want. The Universe must have been determined to use that internet dating site to bring me the romantic love I had been asking for. It's funny how when I let go, was when it happened.

Allowing myself to prosper in the area of relationships has taken years of learning and practicing. And I'm not going to tell you I'm there yet. I continue learning and growing. The key for me was learning how to tap into my inner being and listen. Not only listen, but do what I'm inspired to do, even if it's not what I normally do or have done in the past. Trusting myself this way has opened up so much joy and fulfillment in all my relationships. I've learned to really enjoy my family and friends. I've learned to let adults be adults without meddling into their business with my *perfect advice*. I rarely give advice anymore. I've learned to chill and allow people to be who they really are when they're with me. I believe that's the biggest gift you can give to someone.

Mari Mitchell, CPC is a Certified Life and Relationship Coach, Radio Show Host, Author, Publisher, and founder of Dare to be Authentic.™ Mari is also the author of "Diary of a Hopeless Romantic" and "The Cuban Heart". Her Dare to be Authentic Publishing is the publisher of the "Dare to be Authentic" book series and many other books. Her passion is helping people connect with their authentic self to create a life of joy and fulfillment and bring their authentic talents into the world. Her services are available world-wide via phone, video conference, or in person.

Website: https://www.lifecoachmari.com/

Phone: 954 243-7297

Facebook: https://www.facebook.com/lifecoachmari/

ABOUT THE AUTHOR

Mari Mitchell, CPC is a Certified Life and Relationship Coach, Author, Publisher and Radio Show Host. She's founder of Dare to be Authentic™ and is also the author of "Diary of a Hopeless Romantic" and "The Cuban Heart". Her Dare to be Authentic Publishing is the publisher of the "Dare to be Authentic" book series and many other books. Her passion is helping people connect with their authentic self to create a life of joy and fulfillment and bring their authentic talents into the world. Her services are available world-wide via phone, video conference, or in person.

Made in the USA
San Bernardino, CA
19 January 2020